SCHOLASTIC

TIMES TABLES

Teacher's Book

AGES 7–9

Scholastic Education, an imprint of Scholastic Ltd

Book End, Range Road, Witney, Oxfordshire, OX29 0YD

Registered office: Westfield Road, Southam, Warwickshire CV47 0RA

www.scholastic.co.uk

British Library Cataloguing-in-Publication Data

A catalogue record for this book is available from the British Library.

ISBN 978-1407-18273-5

Printed and bound by Bell and Bain Ltd, Glasgow

Author
Tim Handley

Editorial
Rachel Morgan, Shannon Keenlyside, Audrey Stokes, Helen Lewis and Sarah Sodhi

Cover and Series Design
Scholastic Design Team: Nicolle Thomas, Neil Salt and Alice Duggan

Layout
Claire Green

Illustrations
Gaynor Barrs

CONTENTS

Scholastic Times Tables

The National Curriculum in England expects all children to be taught to recall the multiplication and division facts for multiplication tables up to 12 × 12. From June 2020, all children in England will also take an online timed multiplication tables check, up to and including 12 × 12, at the end of Year 4. This means that, more than ever, a firm grasp of the times tables is key.

It is also important to keep in mind that, for many children, the time spent trying to master the times tables may define how they view themselves as mathematicians. A focus on rapid recall can increase anxiety, not only with multiplication, but with other areas of maths. Conversely, rapid recall of times tables can be confused with deep understanding of multiplication and division; children may move on to new concepts too quickly, causing problems in understanding later on.

These factors make it all the more important that we get right how we teach, and how children learn, the times tables. *Scholastic Times Tables* provides a wealth of rich and varied activities in the *Teacher's Book* and engaging recaps and practice in the *Practice Book*. These work alongside our diagnostic and timed digital practice to help you and your children not only reach National Curriculum expectations but develop a deep understanding of multiplication. The following strategies should be used to get the best results:

Building understanding

- ***Provide opportunities for exploration and reasoning*** *Scholastic Times Tables Teacher's Book* offers a rich variety of activities to get your children thinking about the times tables in a meaningful way. Children should explore ideas, building on what they already know to develop a deeper understanding of multiplication. The *Practice Book* offers varied practice as well as providing further opportunities to develop their problem-solving and reasoning skills (see page 7).

- ***Represent multiplication visually*** When exploring any multiplication table, it is important that children are continually exposed to the different ways in which multiplication can be represented, such as number lines, arrays, counters, number frames, number rods and base-10 equipment. Use these throughout Key Stage 1 **and** 2 as part of your whole-class teaching. Encourage children of **all abilities** to use them to model and check their work as well as explore ideas and patterns.

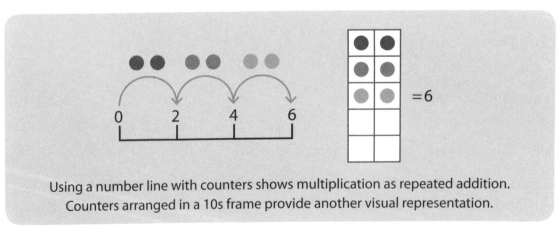

Using a number line with counters shows multiplication as repeated addition.
Counters arranged in a 10s frame provide another visual representation.

- ***Promote talk and discussion*** Many of the activities in this book, as well as the *Practice Book*, ask children to explore an idea and explain their thinking. Shift the focus away from talking only when you think you know the 'right' answer by explaining that talking is a great way to work through a problem as it helps us to work out what we do and do not know. Sharing your ideas with someone else is even better!

- **_Find patterns and draw connections_** Move away from talking about 'tricks' and making things 'easy' (for example _Multiplying by 10? Easy! Put a 0 on it!_) and instead focus on finding patterns and using what you already know to build understanding. Allow children to discover and test these patterns themselves, finding out what works and what doesn't. For example $2 \times 4, 4 \times 4, 8 \times 4$. _What do you notice? Could you use this to predict the answer of_ 16×4?

- **_Use what they know to learn more_** Building on the connections in the tables, we suggest introducing the tables in the following order. Continue to emphasise these links even after all the tables have been introduced.

Key Stage 1			Lower Key Stage 2							
2 ×	5 ×	10 ×	4 ×	8 ×	3 ×	6 ×	7 ×	9 ×	11 ×	12 ×
			(linked to 2 ×)	(linked to 2 × and 4 ×)	(linked to 2 ×)	(linked to 3 ×)	(linked to 6 ×)	(linked to 10 ×)	(linked to 10 ×)	(linked to 10 × and 2 ×)

Developing rapid recall

- **_Practise in short bursts, often_** Rather than devoting a longer chunk of time to rehearsing the times tables, aim to fit short sessions of practice into your day. Even a minute is enough time to fit in a quick all-class chant of a times table.

- **_Make it fun_** Use engaging and low-stress activities to encourage children to commit their times tables to memory, building their confidence and fluency. For example challenge children to set the times tables to music or make up a times tables rap!

- **_Keep it bubbling_** Children will use the times tables across many areas of maths and in everyday life. Continue to revisit even when you think they have learned them by heart.

- **_Consider carefully when to test_** Timed practice can be stressful for many children. Reiterate that understanding is most important and that speed will come with time and practice. Provide opportunities for low-stakes timed practice; this will help them to get used to being tested without the fear of failure. Challenge children to compete against their own personal best time rather than against that of others.

The components

Teacher's Book

The *Scholastic Times Tables Teacher's Book* provides you with a wealth of activities to help your children master the times tables. Work through the activities one by one or dip in and out – whatever works best for you and your class!

Choose from a bank of activities which promote problem-solving, reasoning and fluency. Aim to use a range of activities so that children have an opportunity to approach the times tables in a variety of ways.

The activities use a wide range of resources: some rely on using concrete resources, others have a whiteboard component to them, and others may require a photocopiable resource which can be downloaded from www.scholastic.co.uk/timestables-resources. Finally, some require no resources at all.

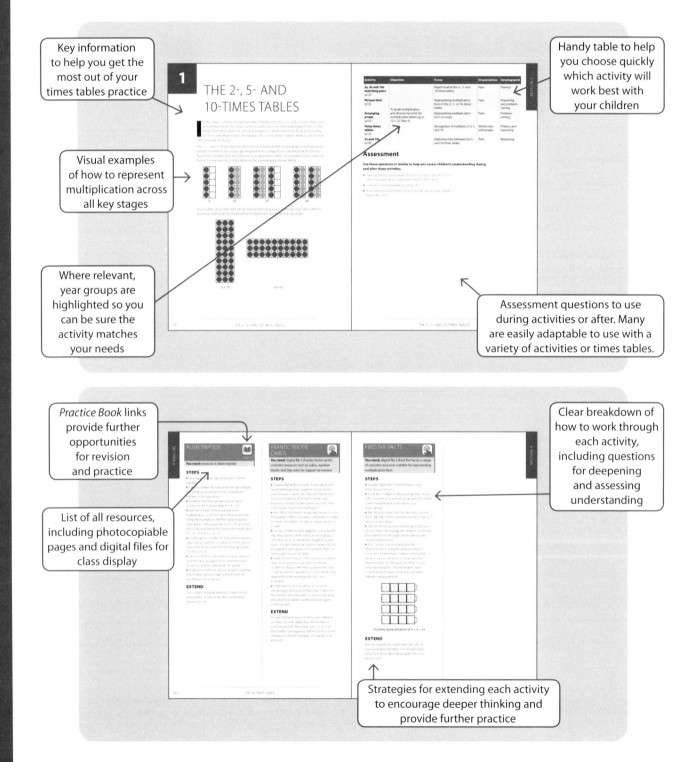

Key information to help you get the most out of your times tables practice

Handy table to help you choose quickly which activity will work best with your children

Visual examples of how to represent multiplication across all key stages

Where relevant, year groups are highlighted so you can be sure the activity matches your needs

Assessment questions to use during activities or after. Many are easily adaptable to use with a variety of activities or times tables.

Practice Book links provide further opportunities for revision and practice

List of all resources, including photocopiable pages and digital files for class display

Clear breakdown of how to work through each activity, including questions for deepening and assessing understanding

Strategies for extending each activity to encourage deeper thinking and provide further practice

The *Practice Book*

The *Scholastic Times Tables Practice Book* has been designed to provide children with further opportunities for revision and practice of the times tables.

Use it alongside the *Teacher's Book*, as part of general class practice or for home learning. Look for the *Practice Book* icon 📖 in the 'You will need' section at the start of an activity for activities which relate directly to the *Times Tables Practice Book*.

Each unit focuses on a different topic or times table.

This section provides children with the opportunity to revisit what they have learned with visual examples to support their understanding.

Children should work through the questions in order for varied practice which builds in difficulty.

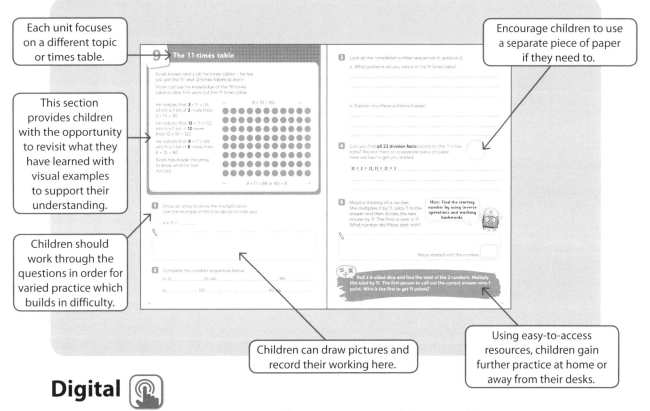

Encourage children to use a separate piece of paper if they need to.

Children can draw pictures and record their working here.

Using easy-to-access resources, children gain further practice at home or away from their desks.

Digital 📱

Additional materials for this book can be found online at the following address: **www.scholastic.co.uk/timestables-resources** these include:

- resource pages including games and worksheets
- supporting PowerPoint digital files for display during your classroom teaching
- quick-fire written tests for additional practice or homework. These tests have three levels of differentiation and are aligned with a unit or group of units from the *Teacher's Book*. Assign one of the three sections at a time and progress through them in order.

If digital files are required, they will be listed in the 'You will need' section at the start of an activity. Look for the digital icon 📱 for activities using digital content.

The digital *Times Tables Check* is included on a USB stick as part of the Classroom Pack, it follows the format of the National Times Tables Check. It can be used to inform your teaching and to provide practice in the test format. Frequently dipping in and out of the program will allow you to gauge progress as well as improving children's familiarity and reducing any associated anxiety that may arise from such checks.

The *Times Tables Check* is customisable, allowing you to select which times tables you would like to include in the check (1–12), the number of questions given and how long children have to complete it. Set up your class then adjust the class settings or individual settings to tailor the check to your children's needs. Use the reporting features to track children's progress and pinpoint areas for additional support. In addition, there is a practice area for children to explore which is not tracked in the reporting area.

The teacher settings are password protected with the password: **login**. A full how to use guide can be found on the USB stick or in the teacher's area of the program.

To install the content, insert the USB stick into a USB port on your computer.
For Windows users, if the install program does not start automatically, navigate to the USB drive, double click the installer program icon and follow the instructions.

For Mac users, navigate to the USB drive and double click the disk image file on the USB drive to mount it. In the window that opens, drag the application file icon to the applications folder icon.

Recommended system requirements:
USB type A port
Windows 7 and later are supported
MacOS 10.9 and above are supported (64bit only)
An internet connection is required for some program features.

Curriculum map

Scholastic Times Tables has been designed to meet the aims of the National Curriculum for mathematics in England to ensure that all pupils:

- become **fluent** in the fundamentals of mathematics, including through varied and frequent practice with increasingly complex problems over time, so that pupils develop conceptual understanding and the ability to recall and apply knowledge rapidly and accurately

- **reason mathematically** by following a line of enquiry, conjecturing relationships and generalisations, and developing an argument, justification or proof using mathematical language

- can solve **problems** by applying their mathematics to a variety of routine and non-routine problems with increasing sophistication, including breaking down problems into a series of simpler steps and persevering in seeking solutions

Mathematics is an interconnected subject in which pupils need to be able to move fluently between representations of mathematical ideas. The programmes of study are, by necessity, organised into apparently distinct domains, but pupils should make rich connections across mathematical ideas to develop fluency, mathematical reasoning and competence in solving increasingly sophisticated problems. They should also apply their mathematical knowledge to science and other subjects.

The expectation is that the majority of pupils will move through the programmes of study at broadly the same pace. However, decisions about when to progress should always be based on the security of pupils' understanding and their readiness to progress to the next stage. Pupils who grasp concepts rapidly should be challenged through being offered rich and sophisticated problems before any acceleration through new content. Those who are not sufficiently fluent with earlier material should consolidate their understanding, including through additional practice, before moving on.

The activities in this book cover the Programme of Study (statutory requirements) in Number: Multiplication and division for the following year groups:

Year 3

Pupils should be taught to:

- recall and use multiplication and division facts for the 3-, 4- and 8-multiplication tables
- write and calculate mathematical statements for multiplication and division using the multiplication tables that they know, including for 2-digit numbers times 1-digit numbers, using mental and progressing to formal written methods
- solve problems, including missing number problems, involving multiplication and division, including positive integer scaling problems and correspondence problems in which n objects are connected to m objects

Year 4

Pupils should be taught to:

- recall multiplication and division facts for multiplication tables up to 12×12
- use place value, known and derived facts to multiply and divide mentally, including: multiplying by 0 and 1; dividing by 1; multiplying together 3 numbers
- recognise and use factor pairs and commutativity in mental calculations
- multiply 2-digit and 3-digit numbers by a 1-digit number using formal written layout
- solve problems involving multiplying and adding, including using the distributive law to multiply 2-digit numbers by 1 digit, integer scaling problems and harder correspondence problems such as n objects are connected to m objects

1 THE 2-, 5- AND 10-TIMES TABLES

I n Key Stage 1, children should have been introduced to the 2-, 5- and 10-times tables, and should enter lower Key Stage 2 being relatively secure in their knowledge of them. In this book, these times tables are used as 'foundation' multiplication tables to work out a range of other multiplication facts. For example the 2-times table is used to work out the 4-times table (through doubling).

The 2-, 5- and 10-times tables should continue to be explored using a range of representations, and the activities in this section are designed to encourage fluency and rapid recall of these foundation multiplication facts. Patterns in multiplication tables can be drawn out by using 10s frames; for example the 5-times table can be represented as shown below.

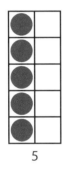 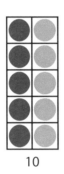 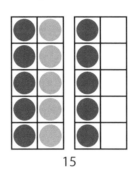 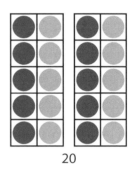

| 5 | 10 | 15 | 20 |

Any multiplication statement can be represented using arrays, which are especially useful for showing commutativity (meaning that multiplication can be done in any order).

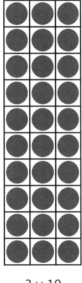

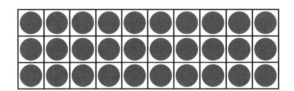

3×10 10×3

Activity	Objective	Focus	Organisation	Development
2s, 5s and 10s matching pairs (p12)		Rapid recall of the 2-, 5- and 10-times tables	Pairs	Fluency
Picture this! (p12)		Representing multiplication facts in the 2-, 5- or 10-times tables	Pairs	Reasoning and problem-solving
Arranging arrays (p13)	To recall multiplication and division facts for the multiplication tables up to 12 × 12 (Year 4)	Representing multiplication facts as arrays	Pairs	Problem-solving
Fishy times tables (p13)		Recognition of multiples of 2, 5 and 10	Whole class and groups	Fluency and reasoning
5s and 10s (p14)		Exploring links between the 5- and 10-times tables	Pairs	Reasoning

Assessment

Use these questions or similar to help you assess children's understanding during and after these activities.

- *Starting from 0, can you count on in 5s? Can you count on in 10s? Which numbers do you say in both counts? Why is this?*

- *Can you count backwards in 2s from 24?*

- *If you start at 0 and count in 2s, will you ever say any odd numbers? Why?/Why not?*

2s, 5s AND 10s MATCHING PAIRS

PAGE 9

You need: resource 1 (2s, 5s and 10s pairs); scissors

STEPS

■ Give each pair of children a copy of resource 1 (2s, 5s and 10s pairs), and ask them to cut out the cards (or pre-cut the cards to save time).

■ Ask the children to place the answer cards (the cards showing a single number) spread out face down on 1 half of the table.

■ Ask the children to place the remaining cards (the question cards) face down on the other half of the table.

■ Children take it in turns to turn over a question card, and then an answer card.

■ If the answer matches the question, the player keeps both cards and has another turn. If the answer does not match the question, the player turns the cards back over, and the other player takes their turn.

■ Play continues until all questions and answers have been matched.

EXTEND

You can develop children's reasoning skills by encouraging them to state which answer card they are looking for after they have turned over a question card. You can also extend the game by asking children to turn over an answer card first, and then state the corresponding multiplication facts that they could be looking for, drawing attention to the commutative law (meaning that it can be done in any order). For example if they were to turn over 30, they could be looking for 3×10, 10×3, 6×5 or 5×6.

PICTURE THIS!

You need: pencils and paper

STEPS

■ Draw a picture on the board to show 2×3. For example you could draw an egg box, 6 soft toys in 3 groups, or 6 aliens arranged in an array.

■ Ask: *What multiplication fact does this picture show? How do you know? Can children identify that your picture shows $2 \times 3 = 6$? Can they explain to their partner how it represents this fact?*

■ Invite children to play the following game in pairs.

■ Each child picks a 'secret' multiplication fact from the 2-, 5- or 10-times table and draws a picture to illustrate it.

■ Once both children have finished drawing their picture, they swap pictures and try to work out each other's secret fact. Ask: *Can you convince your partner that your answer is correct?*

■ If a child is not able to guess their partner's secret fact, then the child who drew the picture shares their secret fact, explains how they think the picture represents this, and asks if their partner agrees.

■ Repeat as time allows. You can add in challenges. Ask, for example: *Can you draw a picture that shows your fact as an array? in groups? as a sequence?*

■ If a particular child needs practice with a key fact, explain that you will be giving them their secret fact, and whisper it into their ear. Play then continues as above.

EXTEND

In order to encourage children to identify the linked division facts that each picture shows, ask: *Does this picture show any division facts? How do you know?*

ARRANGING ARRAYS

PAGES 6 AND 7

You need: counters

STEPS

■ Organise the children into pairs.

■ The first child picks up a random handful of counters, counts them and tells their partner how many counters there are.

■ The second child then arranges these counters into an array based on the 2-, 5- or 10-times table. For example 20 counters could be arranged into a 2×10, 10×2, 4×5 or 5×4 array. Ask: *Is there any other array you could make from these counters?*

■ If the counters cannot be arranged into an array from the 2-, 5- or 10-times tables, they can be arranged into an array from the 1-times table (a straight line of counters). Ask: *Why can't this number be arranged into any other array?*

■ The first child then identifies the multiplication facts shown by the array. This is a good opportunity to reinforce the commutativity of multiplication (meaning that it can be done in any order). Ask: *Does this array show any other multiplication fact?* (Can children identify that a 2×10 array can represent both 2×10 and 10×2?)

■ The second child then takes a random handful of counters, and play continues.

EXTEND

Invite children to explore which numbers of counters must be arranged into a single line (for example 7 counters). Ask: *How many numbers are there that must be arranged into a single line?* You could provide some initial limitation to this question; for example by asking how many numbers would have to be arranged into a single line if you only had 20 counters. You could also encourage children to make any array (for example arranging 12 counters into a 4×3 array) and state the corresponding multiplication facts, as this draws out children's awareness of the relationship between multiplication facts and arrays, as well as providing some exposure to 'new' multiplication facts.

FISHY TIMES TABLES

You need: no resources required

STEPS

■ Explain to the children that they are going to start counting in steps of 1, but each time they say a multiple of 5, they need to replace the number with the word 'fish'.

■ Start counting together as a class in steps of 1. (*1, 2, 3, 4, fish, 6, 7, 8, 9, fish*).

■ Continue counting to at least 60 (12×5).

■ Repeat the game, this time replacing multiples of 2 with the word 'fish' and counting to at least 24.

■ Repeat the game again, replacing multiples of 10 with 'fish', and counting to at least 120.

■ You can vary the game by passing the count along a line or around a circle, so that an individual child says each number, and then the next child in the line or circle says the next number, and so on.

■ If you wish to make the game competitive rather than cooperative, first make sure children are secure with the rules, and then ask them to stand up in a line or a circle. Begin counting by passing the count along the line or around the circle. If a child makes a mistake (for example they say 'fish' when they should not, or they say the multiple of 5 after 'fish': *1, 2, 3, 4, fish, 5*) they are 'out' and sit down. The last children standing are the winners.

EXTEND

Play the version of the game where you pass the count around the circle. If a child has to say 'fish' they are out and sit down. Continue to pass the count around the circle until there is only 1 child left. This child is the winner. Can children predict if they will be out before the count gets to them? Once they are out, can they predict who will win?

5s AND 10s

You need: digital file 1 (5s and 10s)

STEPS

■ Display digital file 1 (5s and 10s) and read the first part of the text together: *Mia thinks there may be a link between the 5-times table and the 10-times table. She has started to write out these times tables side by side.*

■ Ask: *Do you think there is a link between the 5- and 10-times tables?* Invite children to discuss their ideas with a partner.

■ Ask children to write out the 5- and 10-times tables side by side, like the example in the digital file, but continuing up to 12×5 and 12×10.

■ If needed, draw attention to the product of each multiplication. Say, for example: *1 times 5 is 5 and 1 times 10 is 10. Are 5 and 10 linked in any way? Are 10 and 20 linked in the same way?*

■ After some paired discussion time, discuss the question together as a class, drawing out that the 5- and 10-times tables are linked by doubling. (This is a useful link for children to be familiar with, as doubling is used to link other times tables later on in this book.)

EXTEND

Invite children to explore whether there is a link between the 2- and 10-times tables. For example can they identify that the result of multiplying a number by 10 is 5 times larger than multiplying the same number by 2? Children should be encouraged to spot this relationship using 1×2 and 1×10 then 2×2 and 2×10, before checking whether their generalisation applies to other numbers multiplied by 2 and 10. They could do this by using a method for multiplying larger numbers that they are confident with, such as the number line.

MULTIPLICATION STRATEGIES: DOUBLING

Doubling uses children's knowledge of the 2-times table. Doubling can be used to relate the 'foundation' multiplication facts (from the 2-, 5- and 10-times tables) with other multiplication facts and, therefore, it is a key skill for children to maintain.

Doubling can be represented in many ways, including arrays. Number blocks are useful for helping children to understand and visualise why the answer to double a number is always even (as odd + odd = even).

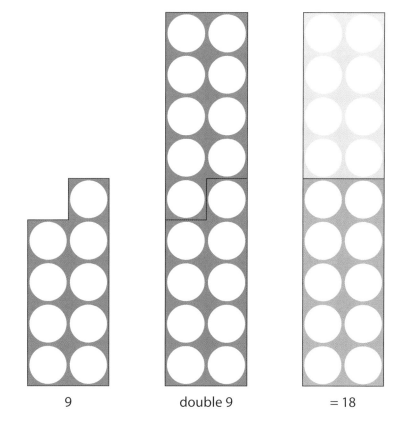

| 9 | double 9 | = 18 |

Children can also use part–whole models and partitioning to help them to double larger numbers. For example the part–whole model below can be used to help children double 36.

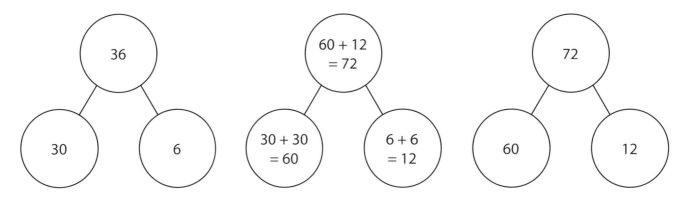

Activity	Objective	Focus	Organisation	Development
Doubling train (p17)		Developing fluency in repeatedly doubling single-digit numbers	Groups of 3	Fluency
Double bingo (p17)	Connect the 2, 4 and 8 multiplication tables through doubling (Year 3)	Doubling numbers up to 25	Whole class or group	Fluency
Double trouble (p18)		Developing fluency in repeatedly doubling single-digit numbers	Groups and pairs	Reasoning

Assessment

Use these questions or similar to help you assess children's understanding during and after these activities.

- *How quickly can you write down the doubles for all numbers from 0 to 10?*
- *Can you complete the gaps in this doubling sequence? 1, 2 , _, _, 16, _, 64*
- *Lily says that doubling is linked to the 2-times table. Is she correct?*

DOUBLING TRAIN

PAGES 11 AND 12

You need (per group): 1 mini whiteboard and pen

STEPS

■ Organise children into groups of 3, sitting or standing in a line.

■ Explain to children that they are in a doubling train, and that they are going to pass the whiteboard down the 'train', doubling the number that is written on it each time.

■ Announce the first number. The child at the front of each train writes it on their whiteboard.

■ The teams then race to pass the whiteboard down the 'train', with each person doubling the number that is written on it. For example if you gave 3 as the starting number, the second person in the line would write 6 and the third person would write 12.

■ Explain that the first team to get the whiteboard to the end of the train (the third person) with the correct answer written on it wins a point.

■ Ask: *What strategy are you using for doubling? Is this the most efficient strategy? How do you know?*

■ After each round, ask children to rotate their position in the train (so that the person at the back becomes the person at the front).

■ Keep playing rounds in the same format, changing the starting number each time. Begin by using starting numbers between 1 and 5, before extending beyond 5. As children rotate their positions in the train each time, you can use the same starting number more than once.

■ When doubling larger numbers, such as 18, remind children about the link between doubling and repeated addition, by asking *What representations could you use to help you double larger numbers?* Encourage children to use physical representations such as a bead string or pictorial representations such as a number line.

EXTEND

Increase the number of people in each train, remembering that for each person added to the train, the number needs to be doubled a further time. 'Trains' with 4 children are useful prior to work on the 8-times table.

DOUBLE BINGO

You need (per child): a mini whiteboard and pen or paper and pencil

STEPS

■ Invite the children to each write down 6 different **even** numbers between 2 and 50.

■ Tell the children these are their 'Double bingo' numbers. When you call out a number that, when doubled, makes 1 of their numbers, they can cross it off.

■ Call out any number between 1 and 25. Children mentally double the number and, if the result is a number they have written down, they cross it off. For example if you call out 15, any child who has 30 written down crosses out 30.

■ Invite the children to consider what numbers they are 'waiting' for you to call. Ask: *What numbers do you need me to call out so you can cross out the numbers you have left on your board?*

■ Once a child has crossed off all their numbers, they stand up and shout 'Double bingo!'. They then explain why they have been able to cross off all their numbers, for example "I was able to cross off 20 because 10 was called out, and double 10 is 20.".

■ You can repeat the game as many times as you like, inviting children to write down new numbers each time.

EXTEND

Children can play the game in small groups with 1 member of the group being the 'caller' and therefore needing to be able to double all numbers to 25 in order to check their group's answers.

DOUBLE TROUBLE

You need: mini whiteboard and pen

STEPS

■ Tell the group they are going to explore what happens when they continue to double a number.

■ Write the number 4 on a mini whiteboard. Ask the children to double this number, and say the statement: *Double 4 is 8.*

■ Ask children to double 8, saying: *Double 8 is 16.* Ask them to continue to double the answer, each time saying the result in the format 'Double…is…'.

■ Continue doubling together until you get over 100 (4, 8, 16, 32, 64, 128).

■ Arrange the children into pairs.

■ Explain that their challenge is to investigate the patterns and relationships when repeatedly doubling numbers. Ask: *Which starting number do you think will get to over 100 in the fewest number of doublings?*

■ Each child in each pair picks a starting number, initially between 1 and 9. They then take it in turns to repeatedly double their number, saying each double in the same format as above. They need to count how many doubles it takes to get over 100.

■ Once children have explored which number between 1 and 9 is the best to choose, change the game. Say that they now need to end up as **close** to 100 as possible and that they can start with any number between 1 and 18. Ask: *Are you able to get exactly to 100 by repeatedly doubling?* Children should notice that they are not able to get to exactly 100. You could then ask: *What is the smallest number you could use to get you to exactly 100 by repeated doubling?* (25)

EXTEND

Invite children to explore patterns in the doubling sequences. Ask: *Do any numbers keep appearing in the doubling sequences? Why do you think this happens?* For example children may notice that 8, 16, 32…etc appear in several doubling sequences, and may be able to explain why this is the case. (If they begin with 2, they will 'click' into the same sequence as the 1 starting with 8, because 2 is linked to 8 by repeated doubling.)

MULTIPLICATION STRATEGIES: USING THE INVERSE

When teaching all multiplication tables, it is important that you encourage children to consider, investigate, use and practise the related division facts.

Multiplication and division are inverse operations. This means that multiplication is the opposite of division, and division is the opposite of multiplication. In other words, division 'undoes' multiplication and multiplication 'undoes' division.

This can be represented using arrays. For example if children know that 3 lots of 6, or 3 × 6, is 18, then they also know that 18 divided into groups of 6 is 3.

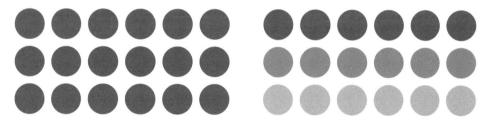

3 lots of 6 or 3 × 6 = 18   18 in groups of 6 = 3 groups or 18 ÷ 6 = 3

Because multiplication is commutative, 3 × 6 = 18 and 6 × 3 = 18, which also means that 18 ÷ 3 = 6.

6 lots of 3 or 6 × 3 = 18   18 in groups of 3 = 6 groups or 18 ÷ 3 = 6

It is important to stress to children that, unlike multiplication, division is not commutative. For example 18 ÷ 3 is **not** the same as 3 ÷ 18.

Activity	Objective	Focus	Organisation	Development
Inverted bingo (p21)	Use place value, known and derived facts to multiply and divide mentally (Year 4); Write and calculate mathematical statements for multiplication and division using the multiplication tables that they know (Year 3)	Using related facts for the 5-times table, including the inverse relationship and commutativity	Whole class	Fluency
Question race (p21)		Using multiplication facts and the inverse relationship to calculate division facts	Groups of 3	Reasoning and fluency
Back to back (p22)	Solve problems involving multiplying and adding (Year 4); Use place value, known and derived facts to multiply and divide mentally (Year 4); Write and calculate mathematical statements for multiplication and division using the multiplication tables that they know (Year 3)	Using the inverse relationship between multiplication and division	Groups of 3	Problem-solving

Assessment

Use these questions or similar to help you assess children's understanding during and after these activities.

■ Can you draw *or make a representation to show the relationship between 2 × 4 = 8 and 8 ÷ 4 = 2?*

■ *How many linked division facts are there for each multiplication fact? Why?*

■ *My answer is 18. What multiplication facts could I be thinking of?*

INVERTED BINGO

You need (per child): a mini whiteboard and pen or paper and pencil

STEPS

■ Invite the children to each write down 6 different numbers between 1 and 12.

■ Tell the children these are their 'Inverted bingo' numbers. They can cross a number off when it is the answer to a question you call out.

■ Call out any question that involves division by 2, 5 or 10, and therefore involves the use of the inverse to calculate the answer. Vary the language you use; for example you may say, *50 divided by 5 is…20 in groups of 2 is…60 shared between 10 is…* In order to check the winner's answers at the end of the game, you may find it useful to record the questions you call (and their answers) as you go along.

■ If children have the answer to the question on their whiteboard or paper, they cross it off and write the statement you called out above the number.

■ Once a child has crossed off all of their numbers, they should stand up and shout, 'Inverted bingo!'. Check to make sure all of their numbers have been called out. Ask them to explain why they have been able to cross off at least 3 of their numbers; for example "I was able to cross off 4, as $20 \div 5$ was called, and 4×5 is 20, so I know $20 \div 5$ is 4."

■ You can repeat the game as many times as you like, inviting children to write down new numbers each time.

EXTEND

Children can play the game in small groups with 1 member of the group being the 'caller' and therefore needing to be able to use a range of language structures relating to multiplication and division.

QUESTION RACE

You need (per child): a mini whiteboard and pen or paper and pencil

STEPS

■ Organise the children into groups of 3.

■ Write a number on the board, that features in at least 1 of the multiplication tables children are familiar with. (12, 24 and 36 can be good numbers to choose.)

■ Give the children 2 minutes to write down on their whiteboards or paper as many different multiplication and division statements as they can that involve this number. For example for the number 24, they could write $24 \div 2 = 12$, $24 \div 6 = 4$, $24 \div 3 = 8$, $24 \div 8 = 3$, $3 \times 8 = 24$, etc

■ While children are working, ask: *Which times tables is this number in? Which multiplication and division facts is it related to? How do you know?*

■ Ask the children to compare their calculation statements with those recorded by the other members of their group, checking that they all agree with each other's statements. Individuals are awarded 1 point for each calculation statement they have written down that neither of the other members of their group have written down.

■ Repeat the activity with a different number. Numbers that appear in multiple times tables are always good numbers to choose. Children compare their statements again, and add any points to the points scored in the last round.

■ Ask: *Which number has the largest number of related facts? How do you know?* Give the children time to discuss this and explain their reasoning.

EXTEND

Children can take it in turns to pick their own number to work from for their group. This work can also form a good maths display, with children putting the focus number in the middle of the paper, and all the related statements around it. Encourage the children to be creative in how they record the calculation statements.

BACK TO BACK

You need (per group): 2 mini whiteboards and pens

STEPS

- Organise the children into groups of 3.
- Ask 2 children in each group to stand back to back, each holding a mini whiteboard and pen. Ask the other child, the 'caller', to stand a few steps away.
- Each of the children standing back to back writes down 1 number from 1 to 12. This can be restricted to the multiplication tables learned so far by giving **1** child in each group a set of numbers to choose from (for example 2, 3, 4, 5, 6 or 10).
- The caller looks at the number on each board, multiplies the 2 numbers together, and announces the answer out loud.
- The players standing back to back race to work out the number the other player must have written down, using the number the caller has called and the number they have written down themselves.
- The first player in each pair to call out the other player's number correctly wins a point.
- Repeat the activity. Rotate within each group, so that each child is the caller once every 3 turns.
- Midway through the session, discuss with children the strategies they are using, drawing upon the inverse relationship between multiplication and division.
- Play for a given length of time, or until 1 player in each group has reached a given number of points.

EXTEND

This activity can be turned into a 'ladder' tournament, with the winner from each pair moving 'up' to the next group each time, and the loser becoming the caller for their current group. The caller from the last game stands back to back with the new person who has joined the group. When the time is up, who is the last person to win a game at the 'top' of the ladder?

THE 4-TIMES TABLE

The 4-times table is likely to be the first new times table children learn in lower Key Stage 2. It is important that children can make connections between the 4-times table and their existing times tables knowledge.

The 4-times table can be linked to the children's existing knowledge of the 2-times table. Numbers in the 4-times table are double (2 times) the corresponding number in the 2-times table.

For example:

$2 \times 5 = 10 \qquad 4 \times 5 = 20 \ (2 \times 10)$

This relationship can be effectively shown using an array.

$2 \times 5 = 10$

$4 \times 5 = 20$ (or 2 lots of 10)

Activity	Objective	Focus	Organisation	Development
4-times table duel (p25)	Recall and use multiplication and division facts for the 3-, 4- and 8-multiplication tables (Year 3); Recall multiplication and division facts for multiplication tables up to 12 × 12 (Year 4)	Developing rapid recall of the 4-times table	Pairs	Fluency
4 in a row (p25)			Pairs	Fluency and reasoning
Alien tripods (p26)	Recall and use multiplication and division facts for the 3-, 4- and 8-multiplication tables (Year 3); Add and subtract amounts of money to give change, using both £ and p in practical contexts (Year 3); Use place value, known and derived facts to multiply and divide mentally (Year 4)	Using related facts for the 4-times table, including the inverse relationship and commutativity	Individuals	Problem-solving and reasoning
Frantic footie cards (p26)		Using and applying the 4-times table and related division facts	Whole class	Problem-solving
Find the facts (p27)	Recall and use multiplication and division facts for the 3-, 4- and 8-multiplication tables (Year 3); Recall multiplication and division facts for multiplication tables up to 12 × 12 (Year 4)	Recognising and creating representations of the 4-times table and related division facts	Partners or small groups	Reasoning

Assessment

Use these questions or similar to help you assess children's understanding during and after these activities.

- *Starting from 0, can you count on in 4s to 48? Can you count backwards?*
- *If you start at 8 and count in 4s will you ever say an odd number? How do you know?*
- *Is it always, sometimes, or never true that the 2-times table is linked to the 4-times table?*

4-TIMES TABLE DUEL

You need (per pair): a pack of playing cards (with kings and jokers removed), or at least 2 sets of 0–12 number cards

STEPS

- Organise the children into pairs.
- Ask each pair to shuffle their cards.
- If you are using playing cards, explain that in this game an ace is worth 1, a jack is worth 11 and a queen is worth 12. It may be helpful to record these values on the board for reference.
- Ask the children to place the cards face down and take it in turns to turn over a card. Partners race against each other to multiply the number on the card by 4, announcing their answer and placing their hand on the card (like in a game of *Snap*). Ask: *What strategy are you using for multiplying by 4? How could you find the answer even more quickly?*
- If the child who is the first to put their hand on the card says the correct answer, they keep the card. If they say the incorrect answer (and their partner spots this) their partner gets the card.
- Keep playing until there are no cards left in the draw pile. You may prefer to set a time limit (for example 3 minutes).
- The player with the most cards at the end of the round wins it.
- You can then repeat, playing further rounds.

EXTEND

This game can be adapted to practise other times tables – children simply multiply the number on the card by the focus times table instead of multiplying by 4.

4 IN A ROW

You need: 10-sided (0–9) dice; resource 2 (4 in a row); counters in at least 2 colours

STEPS

- Organise the children into pairs.
- Give each pair a copy of resource 2 (4 in a row), a 10-sided dice and counters in 2 colours.
- Children take it in turns to roll the dice, and multiply the number they roll by 4.
- If they get the answer correct (and their partner agrees) they place a counter in a square on the resource that contains the answer.
- If they get the answer incorrect (and their partner spots this) their partner places a counter in a square on the resource that contains the correct answer.
- The first player to place 4 counters in a row wins a point. Children then clear the resource and play a new round.
- When children are playing, ask individuals which numbers they are aiming for. Ask them which numbers they need to roll to be able to cover those answers, and how they know this. For example ask: *You say you want to place your counter in this square with 20 in it; which number do you need to roll on the dice to be able to do that? How do you know?* If needed, encourage children to make the link between the 4-times table and dividing by 4.

EXTEND

You could challenge children to make their own '4 in a row' grids for other times tables. They should consider the number placement and whether this affects the chance of winning. Children should realise that, as each number is equally as likely to be rolled, the placement of the answers in the table does not impact the chance of winning.

ALIEN TRIPODS

PAGE 16

You need: resource 3 (Alien tripods)

STEPS

- Give each child a copy of resource 3 (Alien tripods).
- Ask the children to look at the first 'alien tripod'. Ask: *What do you think the link is between the numbers in the spaceships?*
- Establish that the numbers are all linked to a fact in the 4-times table ($8 \times 4 = 32$).
- Ask the children if there are any other multiplication or division facts they could write using the numbers in the first tripod. Establish that, due to commutativity, $4 \times 8 = 32$, and that due to division being the inverse of multiplication, $32 \div 8 = 4$ and $32 \div 4 = 8$.
- Challenge the children to find all the remaining 'alien tripods' with the number 4 in them (that is those that show all the 4-times table facts from 1×4 to 12×4).
- Once a child has completed a tripod, ask them to write the 4 calculation facts that the tripod shows in the box underneath the tripod.
- Invite the children to discuss answers together, and to help convince each other if there are any differences in opinion.

EXTEND

You could investigate tripods for other known times tables, or tripods for the 4-times table beyond 12×4.

FRANTIC FOOTIE CARDS

You need: digital file 2 (Frantic footie cards); concrete resources such as cubes, number blocks and 50p coins for support as needed

STEPS

- Display digital file 2 (Frantic footie cards) and read the first question together: *Frantic footie cards are sold in packs of 4. They cost 50p per pack. Evie has a collection of 36 Frantic footie cards. Assuming Evie has not been given any cards, how many packs of cards has she bought?*
- Ask: *What information do you need to use to solve this problem? What calculation is the problem linked to?* Invite the children to discuss these questions in pairs.
- Discuss children's ideas together, and establish that they need to work out how many groups of 4 there are in 36. Model this together, using cubes, number blocks, or another representation to represent each group of 4. Establish that Evie has bought 9 packs of cards.
- Read the second part of the question together: *How much money has she spent?* Invite the children to discuss with their partner how they could answer this question, and then share ideas, representing the working with 50p coins if needed.
- Invite pairs to work together to solve the remaining problems from digital file 2. Remind the children that they need to ensure that both they and their partner understand and agree on the answer.

EXTEND

Provide further fictional children with different numbers of cards, extending the number of cards beyond 48 (that is beyond 12×4). Can the children use repeated addition and/or other strategies to divide multiples of 4 greater than 48 by 4?

FIND THE FACTS

You need: digital file 3 (Find the facts); a range of concrete resources suitable for representing multiplication facts

STEPS

■ Display digital file 3 (Find the facts). Ask: *What do you notice?*

■ Invite the children to discuss what they notice with a partner or in a small group and then share some thoughts and observations as a larger group.

■ Ask: *What multiplication fact does each picture show? Identify 1 of the multiplication facts that each representation shows.*

■ Ask: *Are there any other number facts that each picture shows?* Encourage the children to identify the related facts through commutativity and inverse relationships.

■ Ask: *Can you create or draw another representation to show the same set of facts?* Once the children have created 1 alternative representation, ask them to create another representation for the same set of facts, and keep repeating this. This will enable them to explore and make connections between different representations.

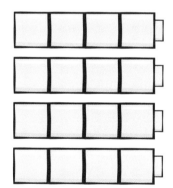

Possible representation of 4 × 4 = 16

EXTEND

Ask the children to create their own sets of representations for other 4-times table facts or for facts from other times tables they are familiar with.

5

THE 8-TIMES TABLE

The 8-times table should be the next new times table that children are introduced to in lower Key Stage 2. This is because children can use doubling to calculate 8-times table facts based on their existing times tables knowledge. Introducing the 8-times table after the 4-times table helps children to appreciate the links between different multiplication tables.

The 8-times table can be linked to children's existing knowledge of the 4-times table. Numbers in the 8-times table are double (2 times) the corresponding number in the 4-times table.

$5 \times 4 = 20$, so $5 \times 8 = 20 + 20$ (or double 20), which means $5 \times 8 = 40$

This relationship can be represented using an array.

$3 \times 4 = 12$

Therefore $3 \times 8 = 24$

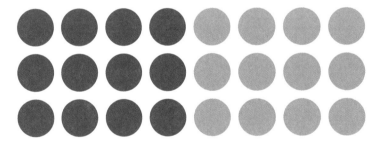

12 + 12 = 24
Remind children that they can use part–whole models, as shown on page 16,
to help them double larger numbers.

Activity	Objective	Focus	Organisation	Development
Crazy 8s (p30)	Recall and use multiplication and division facts for the 3-, 4- and 8-multiplication tables (Year 3); Recall multiplication and division facts for multiplication tables up to 12 × 12 (Year 4)	Building fluency and speed in the 8-times table	Pairs	Fluency
2s and 8s (p30)	Recall and use multiplication and division facts for the 3-, 4- and 8-multiplication tables (Year 3); Use place value, known and derived facts to multiply and divide mentally (Year 4)	Exploring links between the 2- and 8-times tables	Small groups	Reasoning
2, 4, 8 tennis (p31)		Exploring links between the 2-, 4- and 8-times tables	Pairs	Reasoning and fluency
Elegant 8s counting choir (p31)	Recall and use multiplication and division facts for the 3-, 4- and 8-multiplication tables (Year 3); Recall multiplication and division facts for multiplication tables up to 12 × 12 (Year 4)	Exploring related facts for the 8-times table, using the inverse relationship and commutativity	Groups	Fluency and reasoning
Paw print problems (p32)	Recall and use multiplication and division facts for the 3-, 4- and 8-multiplication tables (Year 3); Solve problems, including missing number problems, involving multiplication and division (Year 3); Recall multiplication and division facts for multiplication tables up to 12 × 12 (Year 4)	Creating word problems based on the 8-times table and related facts	Pairs	Problem-solving

Assessment

Use these questions or similar to help you assess children's understanding during and after these activities.

- *Can you count backwards from 48 in 8s? Can you count backwards from 96 in 8s?*
- *Are all the numbers in the 8-times also in the 4-times table? How do you know? Why do you think this is?*
- *Can you give me 3 facts linked to 6 × 8 = 48? How about 3 facts linked to 12 × 8 = 96?*

CRAZY 8s

You need: a polyhedral dice (12-sided ideal, but 10-sided will also work)

STEPS

- Organise the children into pairs.
- Children take it in turns to roll the dice. They then race to call out the answer to the number rolled multiplied by 8.
- The child who calls out the answer first gets 1 point (providing their partner agrees that their answer is correct).
- If the child who answers first makes a mistake, and their partner can give and explain the correct answer, their partner gets the point.
- Draw out the methods children are using by asking: *How did you work out the answer? What facts and knowledge did you use to help you?*
- The winner is the first player to get 10 points.

EXTEND

Increase the number of children playing together. This tends to increase the speed of the game and therefore challenges the players' speed of recall.

2s AND 8s

You need: digital file 4 (2s and 8s)

STEPS

- Organise the children into small groups.
- Display digital file 4 (2s and 8s). Read out the statement: *I think I can use the 2-times table to work out the answers to the 8-times table.*
- Invite the children to discuss this with the members of their group. Bring the class back together and share some of the key ideas from each group.
Ask: *Do you think the statement is correct? How do you know?*
- Once the children have established that there may be a link between the 2- and 8-times tables, ask: *Is this link always true or only sometimes true?* Invite them to investigate this by writing the 2- and 8-times tables alongside each other (for example by writing:
$1 \times 2 = 2$ next to $1 \times 8 = 8$
$2 \times 2 = 4$ next to $2 \times 8 = 16$
and so on).
- Discuss children's thinking with them, establishing that the 2-times table is linked to the 8-times table by multiplying each number in the 2-times table by 4, or by doubling and doubling again.

EXTEND

Give the children a number statement in which you multiply a number greater than 12 by 2 (for example 16 multiplied by 2 is 32). Ask the children to work out the same number multiplied by 8.

2, 4, 8 TENNIS

PAGES 16 TO 18

You need: no resources required

STEPS

- Organise the children into pairs.
- 1 child in each pair says a 2-times table multiplication fact, for example *4 times 2 is 8*.
- The other child has to respond within 15 seconds with the related 4-times table fact, which they can find by doubling the answer to the 2-times table fact, for example *4 times 4 is 16*.
- The first child has to respond within 15 seconds with the related 8-times table fact, which they can find by doubling the answer to the 4-times table fact, for example *4 times 8 is 32*.
- The second child then chooses another 2-times table fact that has not already been used, and play continues as before.
- Encourage the children to notice and use the doubling links between the 2-, 4- and 8-times tables.
- Gradually reduce the time allowed for each response.
- Each time a child makes a mistake that is spotted and corrected by the other child or gets timed out, they 'drop the ball' and their partner wins the point for that game.
- Can the children complete a full 'match' (starting with 1–12 × 2) without anyone winning a point?

EXTEND

Encourage the use of the inverse link between multiplication and division by asking children to start with a division fact linked to the 2-times table (for example *12 divided by 2 is 6*) and then continuing in the same way (for example *24 divided by 4 is 6*, *48 divided by 8 is 6*).

ELEGANT 8s COUNTING CHOIR

You need: no resources required

STEPS

- Organise the children into groups.
- Explain to each group of children that they are a separate 'choir' and therefore need to speak together.
- You are going to be the 'conductor'. When you point at each group, they say an 8-times table fact.
- The first group you point at will say *1 times 8 is 8*, and subsequent groups you point at will say the 8-times table in order, up to *12 times 8 is 92*. Groups should respond quickly when pointed at (conducted).
- Initially, 'point' to each group in turn, but then begin to point to them in a random order, including pointing to the same group twice in a row. Also, gradually increase the speed of your 'conducting'.
- Children may begin to try to predict and have the answer ready for the next times table they think they will be called upon to call. Ask: *How can you increase the speed at which you can respond? Can you work out what the next answer will be before I point at a group?* Encourage children to respond together, so whispered discussions about the next response in between the times they are pointed at is fine.

EXTEND

Replace multiplication facts with division facts linked to the 8-times table. You could also invite a child to be the 'conductor', but they must be able to spot any mistakes the 'choirs' make.

PAW PRINT PROBLEMS

You need: digital file 5 (Paw print problems)

STEPS

- Organise the children into pairs.
- Display digital file 5 (Paw print problems). Explain that the word problems you wrote involving the 8-times table have got mud all over them and you can no longer read them. Ask for the children's help to write some more problems to replace them.
- Write 5 × 8 = 40 on the board. Ask: *Can you help me make up a problem in words that involves this calculation?*
- Give the children time to discuss a possible problem in pairs, and then share some of the problems together. Draw out the key language, such as 'groups', 'sets' or 'lots of' that children have used.
- Give children time to create at least 3 more written problems that involve different multiplication facts from the 8-times table.
- Share some of these problems together. Can the class work out which times tables fact the problem involves?
- Write 40 ÷ 8 = 5 on the board. Ask the children if they can create a word problem that involves this fact. Share some examples together, asking: *How are these problems similar to the ones that involved multiplication? How are they different?*
- Give pairs time to write their own word problems that involve division facts linked to the 8-times table.
- At the end of the lesson, invite pairs to join up into groups of 4 and share some of their problems with each other. Ask: *Which calculation(s) does the problem involve?*
How is it linked to the 8-times table?

EXTEND

Challenge children to create problems that involve multiple steps (for example which require addition before multiplying or dividing by 8).

THE 3-TIMES TABLE

The 3-times table should be the next times table that children are introduced to in lower Key Stage 2.

The 3-times table can be linked to the 2-times table. For example:

Because multiplication is commutative, $2 \times 4 = 4 \times 2$ (2 lots of 4 equals 4 lots of 2).

$2 \times 4 = 8$ (2 lots of 4 is 8)

3×4 is 1 more lot of 4 than 2×4

This can be represented using either repeated addition on a number line or an array.

$2 \times 4 = 8$

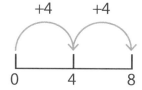 

3×4 (3 lots of 4) is 1 more lot of 4.

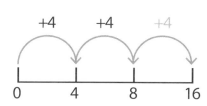 

Because of the commutative property of multiplication, 3×4 is the same as 4×3.

 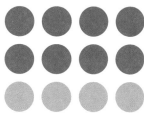

Children can work out any number in the 3-times table by finding out the corresponding number in the 2-times table (using an inverse relationship if needed) and adding another 'lot' of the number they are multiplying by 2. For example to work out 6×3, children can work out 6×2 and add 6.

Activity	Objective	Focus	Organisation	Development
Terrific 3s hoop race (p35)	Recall and use multiplication and division facts for the 3-, 4- and 8-multiplication tables (Year 3); Recall multiplication and division facts for multiplication tables up to 12 × 12 (Year 4)	Fluency in the 3-times table	Groups	Fluency
Evil 18 (p35)		Fluency in the 3-times table	Groups	Reasoning and fluency
Speedy division: 3s (p36)		Exploring related facts for the 3-times table, including the inverse relationship and commutativity	Pairs	Fluency
3 pens (p36)	Solve problems, including missing number problems, involving multiplication and division (Year 3); Recall and use multiplication and division facts for the 3-, 4- and 8-multiplication tables (Year 3); Recall multiplication and division facts for multiplication tables up to 12 × 12 (Year 4)	Solving problems relating to the 3-times table and related division facts	Pairs	Problem-solving

Assessment

Use these questions or similar to help you assess children's understanding during and after these activities.

- *Count in 3s. Do you notice a pattern in the numbers? What do you notice?*
  (Encourage children to look for patterns such as odd/even/odd/even.)

- *Can you use the 4-times table to help you work out the 3-times table? How?*
  (You can use subtraction with a 4-times table fact to work out the corresponding fact from the 3-times table, for example $5 \times 4 = 20$, so $5 \times 3 = 20 - 5$)

- *Which multiplication facts is $33 \div 11 = 3$ linked to? How do you know?*

TERRIFIC 3s HOOP RACE

You need: large 0–9 digit cards; hoops; obstacles for children to negotiate

STEPS

- Go outside or into a large space indoors.
- Organise the children into teams at 1 end of the playing space. Give each team a set of large digit cards.
- Set out the hoops at the opposite end of the playing space; 1 hoop for each team. If you wish, you can also place some obstacles (benches to jump over, etc) between the groups and their hoops.
- Call out a 3-times table question (for example *8 times 3 is…?*). All the children in the team decide on the answer, and then 1 or 2 members of the team race to their hoop carrying the digit cards needed to make the answer and assemble the cards into the answer inside the hoop.
- Each child may only carry 1 digit card, so for 2-digit answers 2 children need to run.
- Award a point to the first team to make the correct answer in their hoop. The children who carried the digit cards then return to their team, taking the digit cards with them.
- Repeat for another 3-times table question, using the commutative law in some of your questions (for example *3 times 12 is…?*).
- Team members should take it in turns racing, so that each child gets an equal chance to take part in the race, but all children in the team are responsible for helping their racers set off with the correct digit cards.
- Ask: *Which multiplication in the 3-times table are you **not** able to answer with the digit cards you have?* (11 times 3)
- Continue playing until either the time is up, or a team has gained a given number of points.

EXTEND

Call out a multiple of 3. Children race with the digit card(s) showing the number they need to multiply 3 by to make the number you called out. (For example if you call 18, children race with the digit card 6.)

EVIL 18

You need: an object to pass around, such as a class mascot or bean bag; a mini whiteboard and pen for every child

STEPS

- Arrange the children standing in a circle, each with a mini whiteboard and pen at their feet. Ensure that the adult leading the game is part of the circle.
- The adult starts the 3-times table count, saying the full fact: *1 times 3 is 3*.
- The count then passes around the circle in the direction chosen by the adult.
- If a child has to say 18, for example *6 times 3 is 18*, they have met 'Evil 18' and are out of the game. They should sit down.
- The count continues, until it reaches *12 times 3 is 36*. The count then reverses, so the next child says *11 times 3 is 33*.
- Each time a player has to say 18 they sit down.
- Players who are sitting down use their reasoning skills to predict who will be the next player to be out, and write their prediction on their mini whiteboard. Ask: *How do you know who will be out next? How quickly can you work it out? Does it matter if the count is going forwards or backwards?* For each correct prediction a player makes (with at least 3 people to go until the person they predict says 18) they gain a point.
- 2 children win the game: the last child standing, and the child who has gained the most prediction points.

EXTEND

Introduce more 'evil' numbers to increase the complexity of the predictions. Other good 'evil' numbers to join 18 are: 3, 30 and 24.
Change the game so that children pass division facts related to the 3-times table around the circle.

SPEEDY DIVISION: 3s

You need: resource 4 (Speedy 3s division cards) pre-cut into cards

STEPS

- Organise the children into pairs.
- Give each pair a set of cards from resource 4 (Speedy 3s division cards), printed onto card if possible.
- Ask pairs to shuffle their cards and place them face down on the table between them.
- Players take it in turns to turn over a card.
- They then race to say a division fact from the 3-times table that starts with the number on the card. For example if the card reads '24', children could say *24 divided by 3 is 8* or *24 divided by 8 is 3* but not *24 divided by 2 is 12*.
- The first player to give a correct division fact linked to the 3-times table wins the card.
- If a player states an incorrect fact or 1 that is not linked to the 3-times table, the other player wins the card.
- Ask: *How do you know which division facts are linked to the multiplication fact? Is there more than 1 possible answer for each multiplication fact? Why is this?*
- Play continues until either 1 player wins all the cards or a time limit is up. If both players still have cards, the player with the most cards wins.

EXTEND

To win the card, a player must state both division facts from the 3-times table that start with the number on the card.

3 PENS

You need: digital file 6 (3 pens)

STEPS

- Display digital file 6 (3 pens). Read the first part of the problem together: P*ens are sold in packs of 3. Mrs James has bought 11 packs of pens for her class. How many pens has she bought?*
- Ask the children to discuss with their partner which number sentence the problem represents.
- Establish that 11×3 is the linked number sentence and that, therefore, Mrs James has bought 33 pens.
- Read out the second part of the problem: *There are 27 children in Owl Class. How many packs of pens will the teacher need to buy for each child to have 1 pen?* Give children time to discuss this question with their partner. Ask: *How is this problem similar to the first problem? How is it different?*
- Establish that this problem is linked to division, that it involves the 3-times table, and that the linked number sentence is $27 \div 3 = ?$ Ask: *Which multiplication from the 3-times table do you need to know in order to work out the answer?* Discuss that it is linked to $9 \times 3 = 27$, so the answer must be 9 packs.
- Share the final part of the problem with children. Ask: *How is the answer to this question linked to the answer to the previous question?* Establish that the teacher will be buying twice as many pens as in the previous question and, therefore, twice as many packs, so they will be buying 18 (2×9) packs.
- Finally, ask the children to work out how many packs of pens you would need to buy for their class. Depending on the number of children in your class, this may provide a good opportunity to discuss interpreting remainders in context (for example if there are 26 children, you would need to buy 9 packs, rather than 8).

EXTEND

Challenge the children to create their own multiplication and division problems linked to the 3-times table.

THE 6-TIMES TABLE

The 6-times table can be linked to the 3-times table by doubling.

$4 \times 3 = 12$ $4 \times 6 = \text{double } 12$

Draw attention to the fact that 6 is **double** 3. Because of this, 4 lots of 6 must be **double** 4 lots of 3. This can be represented using arrays.

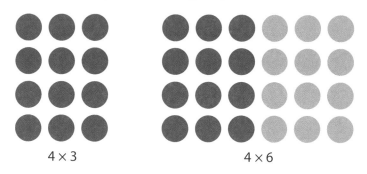

4×3 4×6

The number line can also be used to represent the relationship between the 3- and 6-times tables.

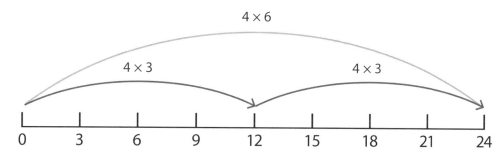

Activity	Objective	Focus	Organisation	Development
6s meet in the middle (p38)	Recall multiplication and division facts for multiplication tables up to 12 × 12 (Year 4)	Related facts for the 6-times table, including the inverse relationship and commutativity	Groups	Fluency
Maths, paper, scissors: all the 6s (p38)		Developing fluency in the 6-times table	Pairs	Reasoning and fluency
Target race (p39)	Use place value, known and derived facts to multiply and divide mentally (Year 4)	Related facts for the 6-times table, including the inverse relationship and commutativity	Groups	Reasoning
The 6-times table museum (p39)	Recall multiplication and division facts for multiplication tables up to 12 × 12 (Year 4)	Representing the 6-times table and related multiplication and division facts	Pairs	Problem-solving and reasoning

Assessment

Use these questions or similar to help you assess children's understanding during and after these activities.

- *Give me a multiple of 6. And another…and another…and another.*
- *Are all the numbers in the 6-times table multiples of 2? How do you know?*
- *Can you create a counting song for the 6-times table?*

6s MEET IN THE MIDDLE

You need: resource 5 (6s meet in the middle), pre-cut into cards

STEPS

- Go outside or into an open space indoors.
- Give 1 card from resource 5 (6s meet in the middle) to each player (including adults if needed to ensure there is an even number of players).
- Ask players to find a partner to 'meet in the middle' and stand facing them.
- Both partners hold up their question so that it is facing the other partner and take it in turns to agree on the answer to each other's question.
- They then swap question cards and meet another person in the middle. Once again, partners answer each other's questions. Each player should already know the answer to the card they are holding, as they agreed on the answer with their previous partner.
- Once both players have answered each other's questions correctly, they swap cards and find another person to 'meet in the middle'.
- Play continues in this fashion.
- It may be useful to introduce a rule that when children are looking for a new partner, they raise their hand – this will help pairs who are ready to 'meet in the middle' find each other.

EXTEND

Invite the children to create their own sets of 'meet in the middle' cards, for either the 6-times table, or all the times tables they are familiar with so far.

MATHS, PAPER, SCISSORS: ALL THE 6s

You need: no resources required

STEPS

- Ask the children if they have ever played *Rock, paper, scissors*. Explain that this is a maths version of the same game.
- Organise the children into pairs.
- Players stand and face each other. Players make fists and say together *Maths, paper, scissors* while moving their fists up and down (as when playing *Rock, paper, scissors*). On the word 'scissors' each player puts out between 0 and 5 fingers.
- Players find the total number of fingers they and their partner have put out and multiply this number by 6. The first player to call out the correct answer wins a point.
- Play for an allotted time period (for example 2 minutes). This game will be fast-paced and energetic!
- After the first battle, invite children to reason about the game. Ask: *Can you work out what the possible answers are based on the number of fingers you put out? Which answers are not possible?*
- Children switch partners and play again.
- Ask the children to evaluate their reasoning. How can they refine it? Establish that if, for example they put out 5 fingers, they know the answer cannot be 6, 12, 18 or 24.
- Children continue to switch pairs, play and review their reasoning.

EXTEND

To win the point, children need to state the full multiplication fact (for example *8 times 6 is 48*) and a related division fact (for example *48 divided by 6 is 8*).

TARGET RACE

You need: mini whiteboards and pens

STEPS

■ Organise children into ability groups. Give each child a mini whiteboard and pen.

■ Write a multiple of 6 on the board (for example 42). This is the target number.

■ Children race to write on their whiteboard a division question that involves both the target number and the number 6 (for example
$42 \div 6 = 7$ or
$42 \div 7 = 6$).

■ The first person in each group to write a correct division sentence wins a point.

■ Repeat the game with a new target number.

■ The game ends either after a set period of time, or when 1 player reaches a predetermined number of points.

EXTEND

Extend some or all groups so that in order for children to win a point, they need to write down both division facts that involve both the target number and the number 6.

THE 6-TIMES TABLE MUSEUM

You need: digital file 7 (The 6-times table museum); a range of classroom objects and mathematical representations; paper and pencil

STEPS

■ Organise children into pairs.

■ Display digital file 7 (The 6-times table museum). Read the first 2 sentences together: *Let's turn the classroom into a museum! Can you create different exhibits that show the 6-times table and its related division facts?*

■ Invite the children to discuss with their partner what 'exhibit' (representation) they could create. Share some of these ideas together and ensure children understand the task. Explain any restrictions on the objects that they can use to create their representations.

■ Give the children time to create at least 4 different representations of facts from the 6-times table and the related division facts. Ask: *What fact are you representing? Can you convince me that your exhibit shows that fact?*

■ Encourage the children to use a range of representations, inducing pictorial representations. Ask: *Could you draw something to show a fact from the 6-times table or a related division fact?*

■ At the end of the session, invite the children to display their exhibits and explore each other's exhibits. Can they identify which multiplication and/or division facts each exhibit shows? Ask: *How is this exhibit the same/different to the ones you created?*

EXTEND

Challenge children to see who can create the most unusual and creative exhibit showing a 6-times table fact or related division fact.

8 THE 7-TIMES TABLE

You can use addition to link the 6- and 7-times tables.

For example:

$6 \times 3 = 18$ (6 lots of 3 is 18) therefore 7×3 is just 1 more 'lot' of 3.

$7 \times 3 = 18 + 3 = 21$

This can be represented using a number line.

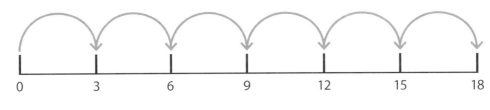

$$6 \times 3 = 18$$

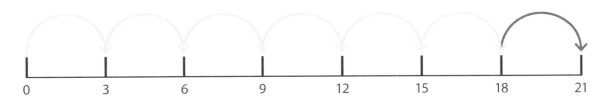

$$7 \times 3 = (6 \times 3) + 3$$

This can be linked to arrays, and therefore the commutative relationship can be seen.

You can easily show that 7 lots of 3 or **7 × 3**... is the same as 3 lots of 7, or **3 × 7**.

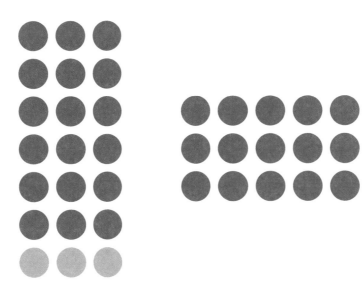

7 × 3   *3 × 7*

Activity	Objective	Focus	Organisation	Development
Snappy 7s (p42)	Recall multiplication and division facts for multiplication tables up to 12 × 12 (Year 4)	Fluent recall of the 7-times table, using the inverse relationship, commutativity and different representations	Pairs	Fluency and reasoning
Single 7s (p42)		Fluent recall of the 7-times table	Groups	Fluency
7 splat (p43)			Whole class or group	Fluency
6, 7, 8 (p43)	Use place value, known and derived facts to multiply and divide mentally (Year 4)	Exploring the relationship between the 7-times table and other times tables	Pairs	Problem-solving and reasoning

Assessment

Use these questions or similar to help you assess children's understanding during and after these activities.

- *Can you write down all the division facts linked to the 7-times table? Who can write them all down the quickest? How are you working systematically to make sure you do not miss a fact?*

- *Are all the multiples of 7 also multiples of any other number? How do you know?* (Multiples of 7 are not all multiples of any other number, unlike all multiples of 8 which are also multiples of 4. This is because 7 is not a multiple of any other number. Note: Children do not yet need to know the term 'prime number'.)

- *Can you create a poster that represents at least 6 facts from the 7-times table?*

SNAPPY 7s

You need: resource 6 (Snappy 7s), pre-cut into cards

STEPS

■ Organise the children into pairs and give each pair a set of cards from resource 6 (Snappy 7s). Explain that the cards show facts from the 7-times table in various ways.

■ Ask each pair to shuffle their cards and share them out between them.

■ Tell the children they are going to play a game of *Snap*. Cards are a 'snap' when they have the same value. If there is a question on the card, its value is the answer to the question.

■ Play as a standard game of *Snap*, with children taking it in turns to turn over 1 of their cards and place it, face-up on a communal pile.

■ When 2 cards are placed on top of each other that have the same value, the first person to shout 'Snap!' and put their hand on the pile wins all the cards in it, but only if they can explain why the 2 cards have the same value.

■ During the game, ask questions to draw out reasoning; for example: *How do you know these 2 cards are/are not equivalent? Convince me. How are these 2 facts linked? What is the relationship between them? What fact would you need to place down next in order for it to be a 'snap'?*

■ If a player calls 'Snap!' when the cards have different values, their partner wins the cards in the face-up pile.

■ Continue playing until 1 player has all the cards. They are the winner.

EXTEND

Ask the children to create a set of *Snap* cards for other times tables, or to focus on specific facts in the 7-times table that they need additional practice with.

SINGLE 7s

You need: no resources required

STEPS

■ Sit the children in a circle, so that they can see each other.

■ Explain that their challenge is to say the 7-times table in order, from $1 \times 7 = 7$ to $12 \times 7 = 84$, as quickly as they can. But there is a twist!

■ Explain that only 1 child is allowed to speak at a time. If 2 children start to speak at the same time, they have to start again, from $1 \times 7 = 7$. If someone makes a mistake (giving the wrong answer or saying a fact out of order) they also have to start again.

■ How long will they need to practise before they can go from $1 \times 7 = 7$ to $12 \times 7 = 84$ without anyone speaking over each other or making a mistake?

■ Encourage the children to discuss and develop strategies.

■ Once they have got used to using 1 strategy (for example they may suggest going around the circle in order, or raising a hand before they speak), change the rules so that the strategy they developed can no longer be used.

EXTEND

Create multiple groups of between 3 and 6 children, each with an adult or trusted 'referee'. Race to see which group can complete the challenge first, without speaking over each other or making a mistake.

7 SPLAT

You need: no resources required

STEPS

■ Go outside or into an open space indoors.

■ Stand in the middle of the space and ask the children to stand in a circle around you.

■ Point at a child in the circle while calling out a 7-times table question (for example *3 lots of 7 is…?, 4 times 7 equals?, What's 21 divided by 3?*)

■ The child you point at ducks and the 2 children either side of them turn to face each other. They both call out the answer to the question, while pointing their hands at the other person.

■ The first player to call out the correct answer 'splats' the other player, and the player who has been 'splat' sits down and is temporarily out of the game.

■ Continue playing; turning, pointing and calling out questions at increasing speed.

■ When 2 players are left, have a '7 splat-off'. The players stand back to back. Call out random numbers, and for each number you call out each player takes a step forward. When you call out a multiple of 7, both players turn, face each other, point and shout, 'Splat!'. The player who is first to 'splat' the other player wins the game.

■ Re-start the game, with all the children being back 'in', and play again.

EXTEND

The winning child could become the '7 Splat Master', taking your place in the middle of the circle and asking the questions, but they need to be able to judge if the answers given are correct!

6, 7, 8

PAGES 28 AND 29

You need: digital file 8 (6, 7, 8); mathematical representations (for example counters, number blocks and number lines)

STEPS

■ Organise the children into pairs.

■ Display digital file 8 (6, 7, 8), explaining that you will first be focusing on the first statement, to find out whether it is true: *I can use the 6-times table to work out the 7-times table.*

■ This statement relates to a strategy you may have taught children when introducing the 7-times table. Ask: *Can you draw or make me something to show whether this statement is true?* Give the children time to work on this together in pairs, and then share their thinking and representations.

■ Read out the second statement: *I can use the 8-times table to work out the 7-times table.* Discuss children's initial thoughts by asking: *What do you think? Is this true?*

■ Give the children time to discuss and investigate this statement in pairs, again asking them to create a representation to show their thinking and reasoning.

■ Ask pairs to share their thinking with the class, establishing that the 8-times table can be used to work out the 7-times table. (For example $8 \times 8 = 64$ so $8 \times 7 = 64 - \mathbf{8}$.)

■ Finally, challenge the children to investigate whether they can use any other times tables to work out answers to the 7-times table. For example can children work out that they can use the distributive law and their knowledge of the 5- and 2-times tables: $5 \times 7 = (5 \times 5) + (5 \times 2)$ or that they can also use the 10- and 3-times tables: $5 \times 7 = (5 \times 10) - (5 \times 3)$?

EXTEND

Challenge children to explore how other pairs of times tables are linked to each other. For example ask: *How are the 8- and 10-times tables linked?* For example $10 \times 8 = 80$ so $8 \times 8 = 80 - (2 \times 8)$ (80 minus 2 lots of 8).

9 THE 9-TIMES TABLE

By the time children are formally introduced to the 9-times table, they should already be able to calculate most of the facts within it by using their existing times tables knowledge and the fact that multiplication is commutative (meaning it can be done in any order).

For example you could encourage children to use the 3-times table to work out that $3 \times 9 = 27$, recognising that 3×9 is equivalent 9×3. You could also invite children to explore the link between the 9-times table and the 10-times table. They should notice that any number multiplied by 9 is '1 lot' of the number less than the same number multiplied by 10. For example: $6 \times \mathbf{10} = 60$ and $60 - \mathbf{6} = 54$ so $6 \times \mathbf{9} = 54$.

The relationship between the 9- and 10-times tables can be represented using arrays or a number line.

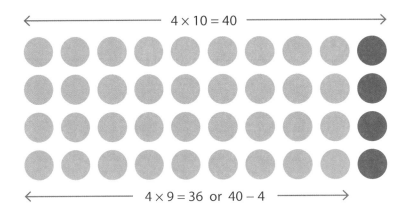

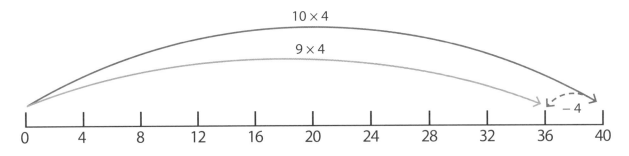

Children may also notice patterns within the 9-times table. One pattern is that the digit root (the sum of the digits in the number, regardless of their place value, until it reaches a single-digit answer) always equals 9. (For example the digit root of 99 is 9 because $9 + 9 = 18$ and $1 + 8 = 9$.) Another pattern is that, for the first 10 multiples of 9, the 10s digit increases by 1 each time (from 0 to 9), and the 1s digit decreases by 1 each time (from 9 to 0).

Whichever patterns you investigate with the children, it is important that you explore the reasons why these relationships exist (because of the link between the 10- and 9-times tables) rather than simply teaching them as 'tricks' without meaning.

10s frames can help children to unpick this relationship.

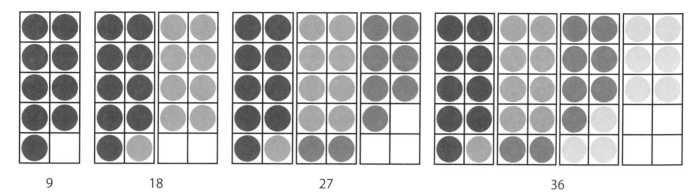

Activity	Objective	Focus	Organisation	Development
Square 9s (p46)		Fluent recall of the 9-times table	Pairs	Fluency
Double-handed maths, paper, scissors (p46)	Recall multiplication and division facts for multiplication tables up to 12 × 12 (Year 4)	Rapid recall and fluency in the times tables from 1 to 9	Pairs	Fluency and reasoning
Racing 9s (p47)		Fluent recall of the 9-times table and related division facts	Groups	Fluency
9s on the money (p47)	Recall multiplication and division facts for multiplication tables up to 12 × 12 (Year 4); Estimate, compare and calculate different measures, including money in pounds and pence (Year 4)	Problem-solving with the 9-times table and related division facts	Pairs	Problem-solving and reasoning

Assessment

Use these questions or similar to help you assess children's understanding during and after these activities.

- *Can you work out the missing numbers in this sequence, which increases by the same number each time?*
  0, ____, ____, ____, 36, ____, ____, ____, ____, ____, ____, ____, ____

- *Which other times table could you use to help you work out the 9-times table?*
  Can you think of another times table you could use? And another?

- *Can you create a poster that will help people remember the 9-times table?*
  What representations will you include? What patterns will you explain?

SQUARE 9s

You need: resource 7 (Square 9s); counters in 2 colours; 12-sided dice

STEPS

- Organise children into pairs.
- Give each pair a copy of resource 7 (Square 9s), counters in 2 colours and a 12-sided dice.
- Explain that resource 7 shows a game board and the aim of the game is to get at least 4 of your counters in a square.
- Children take it in turns to roll the 12-sided dice. They multiply the number they roll by 9, announce the answer to their partner and, if their partner agrees with the answer, place their counter in 1 of the squares on the game board showing that number.
- Ask: *How are you working out the answers? Is there a strategy or pattern you are using?*
- Play continues until 1 child has formed a square out of their counters. This could be 4 counters adjacent to each other in a square, or a larger number of counters that form a continuous square outline around other counters.

EXTEND

In order to place their counter, children need to give both the full multiplication fact and a related division fact.

DOUBLE-HANDED MATHS, PAPER, SCISSORS

You need: no resources required

STEPS

- Ask the children if they have ever played *Rock, paper, scissors*. Explain that this is a maths version of the same game.
- Organise the children into pairs.
- Players stand and face each other. They make 2 fists and say together *Maths, paper, scissors*, while moving their fists up and down (as when playing *Rock, paper, scissors*). On the word 'scissors', each player puts out between 1 and 10 fingers.
- Players race to multiply the number of fingers they have put out by the number of fingers their partner has put out. The first player to call out the correct answer wins a point.
- Play for an allotted time period (for example 2 minutes). This game will be fast-paced and energetic!
- After the first battle, invite the children to reason about the game. Ask: *Why do you think you are not allowed to put out no fingers?* (Because the answer would always be 0.) *What could the largest possible answer be for the number of fingers you have just put out? Why could it not it be any larger? What about the smallest possible answer?*
- Children switch partners and play again.

EXTEND

Play a *Double-handed rock, paper, scissors* tournament: after each 'battle', pair winners with each other. Their previous opponents become their 'cheer squad' and encourage them, as well as acting as umpires and score keepers. In the end, this will result in 2 children battling against each other, with half the class supporting 1 child and the other half supporting the other child.

RACING 9s

You need: large digit cards (0–9)

STEPS

■ Take a group of 10 children outside or into a large space indoors.

■ Give each child a digit card to hold and ask them to spread out around the outside of the playing area.

■ Call out a multiplication from the 9-times table (for example 8 × 9).

■ The children who are holding digits that form the answer (in this case, the child holding the 7 and the child holding the 2) race to the middle of the playing area, and arrange themselves so that they form the answer.

■ The rest of the children shout out the completed fact (for example 8 × 9 = 72) while the children who have come to the middle race to get back to their original position before the rest of the children have finished shouting out the completed fact.

■ Repeat, including questions that involve the commutative property (for example 9 × 11) and division (for example 63 ÷ 9).

EXTEND

Introduce other groups of 10 children, giving each group their own set of digit cards. Each group of 10 children is now a team. Play in the same way as before, but this time teams race to be the first to make the answer with the digit cards.

9s ON THE MONEY

You need: digital file 9 (9s on the money)

STEPS

■ Organise the children into pairs.

■ Display digital file 9 (9s on the money), reading the first part of the problem together: *At 99s American Diner a child's meal deal costs £9. Mrs Hammond and her 4 children went to dinner at 99s American Diner. Mrs Hammond's meal cost £18 and each of her children had a child's meal deal. How much did their food cost altogether?*

■ Ask the children to discuss this problem in pairs. Ask: *Does the problem involve 1 or 2 steps? Which number sentences are linked to this problem? How do you know?*

■ Discuss the children's thinking together. Explore the steps involved in solving the problem (first working out how much the children's food costs, then adding £18) and, therefore, which number sentences are involved in the problem.

■ Invite the children to work out the solution to the problem, sharing their steps and thinking with their partner.

■ Read the second part of the problem together: *The next Sunday, the diner took £108 from children's meal deals. How many children had a meal deal that day?* Ask: *Can you work out the number sentence needed to solve this problem? How do you know?*

■ Ask the children to solve the second part of the problem in pairs.

■ Finally, invite the children to create their own word problems that involve the 9-times table and related division facts.

EXTEND

Challenge the children to create multi-step problems involving the 9-times table and related division facts.

10

THE 11-TIMES TABLE

Encourage children to use their existing times tables knowledge and the commutative property of multiplication to work out the majority of the 11-times table.

You should also encourage children to explore the link between the 11- and 10-times tables. For example using the commutative property, they may notice that $4 \times 11 = 44$, which is 1 lot of **4** more than $4 \times 10 = 40$. This relationship can be presented using an array.

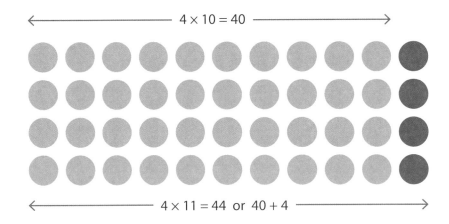

Encourage children to appreciate that they can use their knowledge of the 10-times table in this way to work out any fact from the 11-times table.

Children may also notice patterns within the 11-times table. For example it is common for children to state that "You put the number you are multiplying by twice." by which they mean, for example that 3×11 is **33**. However, it is important for children to explore why this pattern exists. (Because 10 times a number is always a multiple of 10, 11 times the same number will always be the multiple of 10 plus the number you are multiplying by, which creates the 'double digit' effect for the first 9 multiples of 11.)

Children should also investigate at what point any pattern they notice breaks down. For example 11×11 is not 1111, which is a common answer if children have not developed the conceptual understanding behind the pattern.

Activity	Objective	Focus	Organisation	Development
Geo 11 (p50)	Recall multiplication and division facts for multiplication tables up to 12 × 12 (Year 4)	Related facts for the 11-times table, including using the inverse and commutativity, and exploring representations for these facts	Pairs or independent	Fluency and problem-solving
Double digits (p50)	Recall multiplication and division facts for multiplication tables up to 12 × 12 (Year 4); Use place value, known and derived facts to multiply and divide mentally (Year 4)	Using and applying the 11-times table and related division facts	Pairs	Reasoning
Who will be elevenses for sharks? (p51)	Recall multiplication and division facts for multiplication tables up to 12 × 12 (Year 4)	Related facts for the 11-times table, including using the inverse	Whole class	Fluency

Assessment

Use these questions or similar to help you assess children's understanding during and after these activities.

- *What is 24 times 11? How did you work out the answer?*
- *Can you write a word problem for your partner that they need to use their knowledge of the 11-times table to solve?*
- *Can you create a poem that will help people remember the 11-times table?*

GEO 11

PAGE 36

You need: 11 × 11 geoboards; elastic bands

STEPS

- Depending on the resources available, organise the children into pairs or let them work on their own.
- Give each child (or pair of children) a geoboard and 4 elastic bands.
- Call out either a multiple of 11 or a multiplication from the 11-times table (without the answer).
- Children use elastic bands to create an array on the geoboard that represents the number or multiplication you called out. (For example if you call out 66, children make a 6 × 11 or 11 × 6 array.)
- Children then discuss with another child or pair (comparing geoboards) and check their answers with each other, making sure they both agree. Ask: *How do you know this is an array for this number/multiplication? How could you quickly check? Encourage children to check whether the array shows the correct number by counting the number of pegs down the side and across the top of the array and multiplying them together.*
- Repeat, calling out another multiple of 11 or multiplication from the 11-times table.
- Encourage the children to consider both arrays they could make for a given multiple. Ask: *Is there another array you could make? Why does this still show the number?*

EXTEND

Once children have made an array, encourage them to give 2 multiplication facts and 2 division facts for it.

DOUBLE DIGITS

You need: digital file 10 (Double digits); 10s frames; number blocks; number lines

STEPS

- Organise the children into pairs.
- Display digital file 10 (Double digits), reading together the text inside the speech bubble: *To answer any 11-times table question you just write the number you are multiplying by 11 twice. So if you are working out 4 × 11, you just write 4 twice, making 44.*
- Ask the children whether the statement is always, sometimes or never true, and encourage them to discuss their ideas in pairs.
- Share the children's initial thinking together, discussing as a class. Establish that the statement is only sometimes true. Ask: *When does the pattern* **not** *apply?*
- Ask the children to work out with their partner why the pattern works from 1 × 11 to 9 × 11, but does not work for 10 × 11, 11 × 11 or 12 × 11. Encourage them to represent the times table facts in different ways, including 10s frames, number blocks and number lines, exploring the link between the 11-times table and the 10-times table.
- After a period of paired exploration, discuss the patterns children have noticed together as a class.

EXTEND

Can children extend the pattern they have noticed for the 11-times table to the related division facts? For example ask: *How could you use the pattern to work out 99 ÷ 9? Why does the pattern work?*

WHO WILL BE ELEVENSES FOR SHARKS?

PAGE 37

You need: 12 hula hoops; number cards 1–12

STEPS

- Go outside or into a large space indoors.
- Place the hoops around the space, placing the number cards 1–12 next to each hoop, so each hoop has a number.
- Tell the children they are swimmers and their aim is not to get eaten by sharks! Explain that the sharks eat anyone who is in the hoop with the number you have to multiply by 11 to make the number you call out.
- Ask the children to run around the space. After a while, call out *Sharks!* Children have 5 seconds to stand inside a hoop. If a hoop is full, they must find another hoop.
- Once the 5 seconds is up and all the children are standing in a hoop, call out a multiple of 11 (for example 99). Children work out which number is multiplied by 11 to make 99, and shout together, for example: *9 times 11 is 99, so the sharks eat number 9!* Ask: *How can you work out the number you multiply by 11 to get this answer? Which operation and relationships are you using?*
- Any children standing in the hoop with the number you need to multiply by 11 to make the number you called are out. When children are out, they sit out, but they still need to join in with the whole class 'shout'.
- Invite children to move around the space again and continue play as above.
- Part way through the game, change what children need to shout out to a division statement (for example *99 divided by 11 is 9, so the sharks eat number 9!*).
- The last child remaining wins.

EXTEND

Can children reason about which numbers they are picking? Children may initially think some numbers are better to choose than others. Explore this with them, helping them to work out whether all multiples of 11 (up to 132) have an equal chance of being called.

11 THE 12-TIMES TABLE

The 12-times table is often the last times table introduced in lower Key Stage 2. Encourage children to appreciate that, due to the commutative property of multiplication (meaning that it can be done in any order), they can work out all but 1 of the 12-times table facts by using times tables facts they already know. For example 9×12 can be solved using knowledge of 12×9.

Children should realise that 12×12 is the only 'new' multiplication fact in the 12-times table. Encourage them to use their existing times-table knowledge to work out the answer.

With an understanding of the distributive property of multiplication, children can write 12×12 as, for example $(12 \times 10) + (12 \times 2)$. They can then work out that $12 \times 12 = 120 + 24 = 144$. This can be represented using an array.

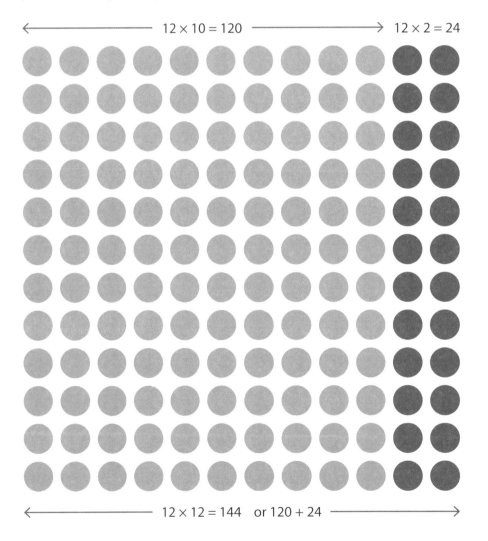

$\longleftarrow$ $12 \times 10 = 120$ $\longrightarrow$ $12 \times 2 = 24$

$\longleftarrow$ $12 \times 12 = 144$ or $120 + 24$ $\longrightarrow$

Activity	Objective	Focus	Organisation	Development
Terrific 12s (p54)	Recall multiplication and division facts for multiplication tables up to 12 × 12 (Year 4)	Fluency in the 12-times table	Small groups or pairs	Fluency
Multiples clock (p54)		Related division facts for the 12-times table	Whole class or groups	Fluency
Looping 12s (p55)	Recall multiplication and division facts for multiplication tables up to 12 × 12 (Year 4); Use place value, known and derived facts to multiply and divide mentally (Year 4)	Related facts for the 12-times table, including related division facts	Whole class or large group	Fluency and reasoning
Anyone for tennis? (p55)	Recall multiplication and division facts for multiplication tables up to 12 × 12 (Year 4); Use place value, known and derived facts to multiply and divide mentally (Year 4); Solve problems involving multiplying and adding (Year 4)	Problem-solving with the 12-times table and related division facts	Pairs	Problem-solving

Assessment

Use these questions or similar to help you assess children's understanding during and after these activities.

- *How can you use facts from other times tables to help you with the 12-times table?*
- *How quickly can you write the first 12 multiples of 12, in order?*
  Cover what you have just written. How quickly can you write the list backwards, starting at 144?
- *What patterns do you notice in the 12-times table?*

TERRIFIC 12s

You need: 12-sided dice; mini whiteboards and pens

STEPS

■ Organise the children into pairs or small groups, giving each pair or group a 12-sided dice and a mini whiteboard and pen.

■ Children take it in turns to roll the dice.

■ All children in the pair or group then multiply the number on the dice by 12 and call out the answer.

■ If the first person to call out an answer is correct (and the rest of the group agrees), the answer becomes the start of their score, which they record on the mini whiteboard.

■ Play continues and each time a player wins, they add the answer to their score.

■ If the first person to call out an answer is incorrect, the other player(s) add the correct answer to their score(s).

■ Encourage the children to consider the methods they are using to calculate their answers. Ask: *How are you working out your answers? Are you using any other times tables facts to help you?*

■ The winner is the first person whose score totals over 1000.

EXTEND

To win points, children have to state the whole family of multiplication and division facts related to the dice roll. For example rolling an 8, they would need to call out:

$8 \times 12 = 96$

$12 \times 8 = 96$

$96 \div 12 = 8$

$96 \div 8 = 12$

MULTIPLES CLOCK

You need: a set of large 0–12 number cards

STEPS

■ Go outside or into a large space indoors.

■ Place the number cards in order in a circle around the outside of the playing area to form a 'clock face'.

■ Call out a multiple of 12 (up to 144).

■ Children run to the number that makes the number you called out when multiplied by 12. For example if you call out 108, the children run to the number 9.

■ Once all the children are at the correct number, they say the multiplication fact out loud together (for example *9 times 12 is 108*).

■ Children then return to the centre of the playing area and you call out another multiple of 12.

■ Encourage the children to explain their thinking and reasoning. Ask: *How do you know that the answer is (x)? How are you working out which number you need to run to? How is this linked to the 12-times table?*

EXTEND

Ask children to chant both a multiplication fact and a division fact each time (for example *9 times 12 is 108; 108 divided by 12 is 9*).

LOOPING 12s

You need: resource 8 (Looping 12s) pre-cut into cards

STEPS

■ Organise the children into a group of no more than 24

■ Shuffle the cards cut out from resource 8 (Looping 12s) and distribute them, so that each child has at least 1 card.

■ Each card has 2 parts: an answer ('I have…') and a question ('Who has…?').

■ Pick a child to start. They read out the 'Who has…?' question on their card (for example *Who has 60 divided by 5?*) The child who has the answer to this question on the 'I have…' part of their card reads it out (for example *I have 12.*) followed by their 'Who has…?' question.

■ Play continues, until the person who read out the first question reads out their 'I have…' answer. This should be when all of the cards have been used and the 'loop' has been completed.

■ Once children are familiar with the game, introduce a time challenge. Ask: *How quickly can you complete the loop? Can you improve on your time from before?*

EXTEND

Organise the children into 2 groups, each with a complete set of the cards from resource 8. Both groups start at the same time and race against each other to see who can complete their loop first.

ANYONE FOR TENNIS?

You need: digital file 11 (Anyone for tennis?)

STEPS

■ Display digital file 11 (Anyone for tennis?), reading out the first problem: *A standard outdoor tennis court is 11 metres wide. There must be at least half a metre of empty space on either side of the court before the space for the next court starts. Tuckswood High School has a space 72 metres wide on which they want to build some tennis courts. How many courts can they fit in?*

■ Ask the children to discuss this problem in pairs. Ask: *What information do you need from the problem? Are 1 or 2 steps needed to solve this problem? Which times table is involved?*

■ Discuss the children's ideas. Establish that they first need to work out the width needed per court. Discuss that this is 11 metres plus 2 lots of half a metre, so each court needs 11 metres + 1 metre of space. Ensure children make the link between the total width needed for each court (12 metres) and the 12-times table.

■ Give the children time to solve the problem in pairs. Ask: *Which multiplication or division facts are you using? Then discuss the answer together as a class.*

■ Share the second problem: *Methwold High School wants to build 12 tennis courts. What width of space do they need to place the courts: a. in a single row? b. in 2 rows? c. in 3 rows?*

■ Give children time to discuss and solve the problem in pairs. Encourage them to make sketches to help them visualise the arrangement of the courts and, therefore, the total space needed. Ask, for example: *If the 12 courts are in 2 rows, how many courts will be in each row? How much space is needed?*

■ Ask pairs to join up to form groups of 4. Ask them to compare answers to the second problem – do they agree with each other? If they disagree, can they find and correct the error?

EXTEND

If you have a large outdoor space, arrange for children to measure the width of this space and work out how many tennis courts could fit in it.

12 MIXED TIMES TABLES PRACTICE

Once children have learned all of the times tables, it is important that they maintain fluency. Rapid recall of multiplication facts will help children when they begin to multiply larger numbers (using informal or formal methods) and when they calculate with decimal numbers and multiples of 10, 100 and 1000.

While some of the activities from the other sections of this book recap and use times tables knowledge that has been developed so far (or can be adapted to do so), this section includes a selection of activities that involve all of the times tables.

Activity	Objective	Focus	Organisation	Development
All out skirmish (p58)	Recall multiplication and division facts for multiplication tables up to 12 × 12 (Year 4)	Rapid recall of all times table facts up to 12 × 12	Pairs	Fluency
Digit race (p58)	Recall multiplication and division facts for multiplication tables up to 12 × 12 (Year 4); Use place value, known and derived facts to multiply and divide mentally (Year 4)	Rapid recall of all times table facts up to 12 × 12	Groups	Fluency
Fizzbuzz (p59)	Recall multiplication and division facts for multiplication tables up to 12 × 12 (Year 4)	Recall and recognition of numbers in the 1- to 12-times tables, including common multiples	Whole class or groups	Reasoning and fluency
Mystery times tables (p59)	Recall multiplication and division facts for multiplication tables up to 12 × 12 (Year 4); Use place value, known and derived facts to multiply and divide mentally (Year 4); Solve problems involving multiplying and adding (Year 4)	Identifying patterns within the times tables	Individuals	Problem-solving and reasoning

Assessment

Use these questions or similar to help you assess children's understanding during and after these activities.

- *Which times tables do you find the easiest? The hardest? Why do you think this is? What strategies could you develop to help you become more secure in your knowledge of the times tables you find the hardest?*

- *Which times table is the number 42* (or any other number) *in?*

- *Which number below 100 is in the most times tables?*

- *Can you represent 4 × 7? Can you give me another representation for the same fact? And another?*

- *Kelly says, "Every multiplication fact has 3 other related facts." Is she correct?* (No, because multiplication facts in which a number is multiplied by itself, such as 4 × 4, have only 1 related fact: 16 ÷ 4 = 4)

ALL OUT SKIRMISH

You need (per pair): a pack of playing cards (with kings and jokers removed)

STEPS

- Organise the children into pairs, giving each pair a pack of playing cards.
- Ask each pair to shuffle their cards and divide them into 2 face-down piles, 1 pile per child.
- Explain that in this game an ace is worth 1, a jack is worth 11 and a queen is worth 12. It may be helpful to record these values on the board for reference.
- Both partners simultaneously turn over the card from the top of their pile. Partners race against each other to multiply the numbers on the 2 cards together and call out the answer.
- If the child who calls out the answer first gets it correct, they keep both cards. If they call out the incorrect answer (and their partner spots this) their partner gets the cards.
- Keep playing until 1 player has no cards left. You may prefer to set a time limit (for example 3 minutes).
- The player with the most cards at the end of the round wins it.
- Encourage children to consider how they are calculating each multiplication. Ask: *How are you working out your answers? Are any times tables easier to work out than others? Which times tables can you answer the quickest?*
- You can then repeat, playing further rounds.

EXTEND

Change the value of the picture cards to increase the focus on certain times tables. For example if the 8-times table is still an area of weakness, you could reinsert the kings, and make both aces and kings worth 8, increasing the likelihood that children will need to answer a question based on the 8-times table.

DIGIT RACE

You need: large digit cards (0–9); sticky tack; objects to act as obstacles

STEPS

- Go into a large space indoors.
- Organise the children into teams, asking them to spread out along 1 end of the playing space. Give each team a set of large digit cards with sticky tack on the back.
- Set out an obstacle course for each team (for example hoops to go under, benches to cross, etc) Make the course similar for each team so that the game is fair.
- Call out a times tables question. All the children in each team decide on the answer and then a child or children from the team race the digit cards needed to make the answer through the obstacle course and stick them on the wall at the opposite end of the playing space.
- Each child may only carry 1 digit card, so for 2-digit answers 2 children need to race and for 3-digit answers 3 children need to race.
- Award a point to the first team to make the correct answer on the wall. Children return to their team, taking the digit cards with them.
- Repeat with another times tables question. Children should take it in turns racing, so that each child gets an equal chance to take part in the race, but all members of the team are responsible for helping their 'racers' set off the with correct digit cards.
- Ask: *Is there any multiplication you would not be able to answer with the digits you have?* (Any multiplication whose answer has repeated digits.)
- Continue playing until either a set time is up, or a team has won a pre-determined number of points.

EXTEND

Give each team another 2 sets of digit cards, so that it is possible to make all the answers in the 1- to 12-times tables.

FIZZBUZZ

You need: no resources required

STEPS

■ Tell the children they are going to count in steps of 1, but each time they say a multiple of 3, they need to replace the number with the word 'fizz'.

■ Count together in steps of 1 to at least 36. (*1, 2, fizz, 4, 5, fizz, 7, 8, fizz, 10…*) Repeat, this time replacing multiples of 4 with the word 'buzz' and counting to at least 48.

■ Tell the children they are going to combine the 2 counts (replacing multiples of 3 with 'fizz' and multiples of 4 with 'buzz'.) Ask: *Which numbers would you say both fizz and buzz (fizzbuzz) for? How many times do you think we will say fizzbuzz if we count to 50?* Count to 50 in this way and find out.

■ You can vary the game by passing the count along a line or around a circle, so that an individual child says each number and then the next child in the line or circle says the next number, and so on.

■ Once children are familiar with the game, ask: *Which pairs of numbers make the most fizzbuzzes (have the most common multiples)? Which make the least? How do you know?* Give children time to work on these questions in small groups before sharing their ideas, and then pick 1 or more pairs of numbers they suggest and play the game with these numbers to test their reasoning.

EXTEND

Play the version of the game where you pass the count around the circle. If a child has to say 'fizzbuzz' they are out and sit down. Continue to pass the count around the circle until there is only 1 child left. Can children predict if they will be out before the count gets to them? Once they are out, can they predict who will win?

MYSTERY TIMES TABLES

You need: resource 9 (Mystery times tables)

STEPS

■ Organise the children into pairs and give each pair a copy of resource 9 (Mystery times tables). Ask them to look at the sheet for a minute and discuss what they think the challenge you are about to give them could be.

■ Explain that this puzzle is made up of 2 different multiplication tables in which the digits have been replaced by letters. To solve the puzzle, they need to work out which digit each letter stands for. To make the task more challenging, the multiplication sentences in the second times table are not written in order.

■ Ask the children to discuss with their partner different approaches they could take to work out which digit each letter stands for.

■ Share ideas together. Ask: *In Set 1, how many answers are below 10? How do you know? What does this tell you about the times table? Can you spot the multiplication that is 11 times something? How do you know?* (By looking for the repeated letter.) *Can you work out which letter stands for the digit 1? Can you spot a number multiplied by itself? What does this tell you about its answer?*

■ Give pairs time to work on attempting to solve Set 1.

■ Ask each pair to join another pair and to share their working and answers. Do both pairs agree with each other's solution?

■ Ask the children to work with their partner to solve Set 2, explaining that it has a new set of letters, but that each letter still stands for a digit between 0 and 9.

EXTEND

Challenge pairs to create their own mystery times tables puzzle for another pair to solve. This could open up discussion around which are the easiest/ hardest multiplication tables to identify, and why.

NOTE Set 1: M = 6; N = 1; P = 5; Q = 3; R = 9; S = 4; T = 2; V = 0; Y = 8; Z = 7
Set 2: A = 9; B = 0; C = 1; D 3; E = 5; F = 8; G = 7; J = 2; K = 6; L = 4

12 × 12 TIMES TABLES SQUARE

	1	2	3	4	5	6	7	8	9	10	11	12
1	1	2	3	4	5	6	7	8	9	10	11	12
2	2	4	6	8	10	12	14	16	18	20	22	24
3	3	6	9	12	15	18	21	24	27	30	33	36
4	4	8	12	16	20	24	28	32	36	40	44	48
5	5	10	15	20	25	30	35	40	45	50	55	60
6	6	12	18	24	30	36	42	48	54	60	66	72
7	7	14	21	28	35	42	49	56	63	70	77	84
8	8	16	24	32	40	48	56	64	72	80	88	96
9	9	18	27	36	45	54	63	72	81	90	99	108
10	10	20	30	40	50	60	70	80	90	100	110	120
11	11	22	33	44	55	66	77	88	99	110	121	132
12	12	24	36	48	60	72	84	96	108	120	132	144

12 × 12 BLANK TIMES TABLES SQUARE

	1	2	3	4	5	6	7	8	9	10	11	12
1												
2												
3												
4												
5												
6												
7												
8												
9												
10												
11												
12												

100 SQUARE

1	2	3	4	5	6	7	8	9	10
11	12	13	14	15	16	17	18	19	20
21	22	23	24	25	26	27	28	29	30
31	32	33	34	35	36	37	38	39	40
41	42	43	44	45	46	47	48	49	50
51	52	53	54	55	56	57	58	59	60
61	62	63	64	65	66	67	68	69	70
71	72	73	74	75	76	77	78	79	80
81	82	83	84	85	86	87	88	89	90
91	92	93	94	95	96	97	98	99	100

NUMBER WALL 4

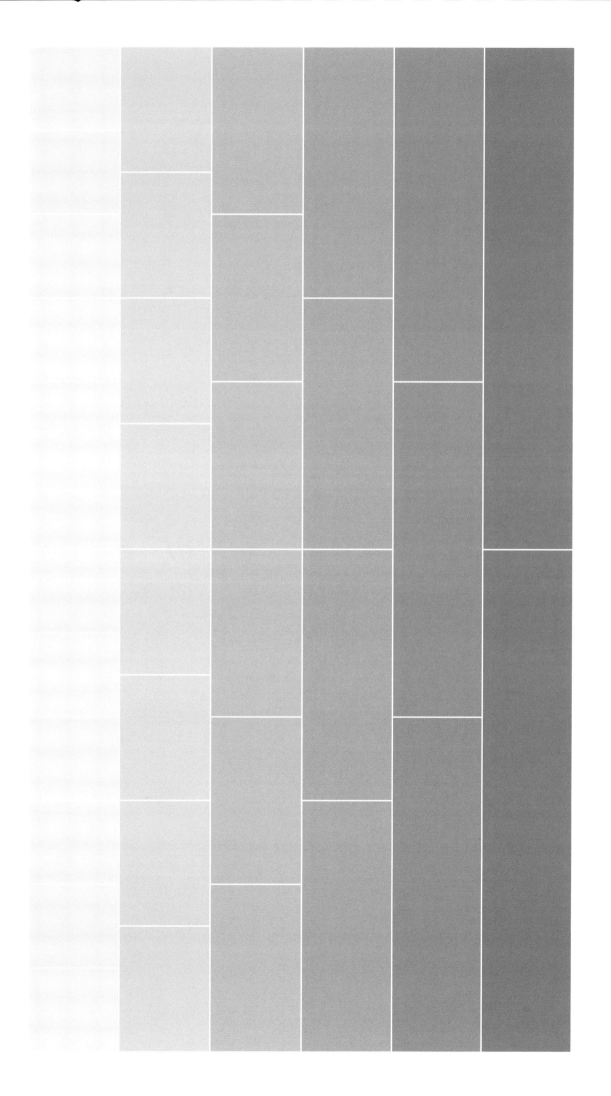

QUICK TESTS FOR SATs SUCCESS

BOOST YOUR CHILD'S CONFIDENCE WITH 10-MINUTE SATs TESTS

- Bite-size mini SATs tests which take just 10 minutes to complete
- Covers key National Test topics
- Full answers and progress chart provided to track improvement
- Available for Years 1 to 6

Find out more at www.scholastic.co.uk